BEGINNER'S GUIDE TO
WHISKEY

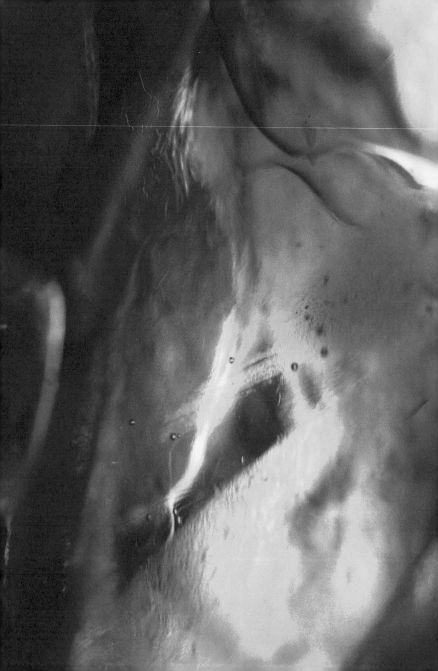

BEGINNER'S GUIDE TO
WHISKEY

Traditions, Types & Tastes
of the Ultimate Spirit

SAM GREEN

BOURBON STEWARD AND WHISKEY SOMMELIER

R
ROCKRIDGE
PRESS

Interior and Cover Designer: Michael Patti
Art Producer: Michael Hardgrove
Editor: Sean Newcott
Production Editor: Andrew Yackira

Illustration © Essi Kimpimaki, 2019

Photography © Getty Images/kcline, cover; Shutterstock/palmclassical, pp. ii, 127; Shutterstock/Leszek Czerwonka, pp. iv, v; Shutterstock/The Len, pp. vi, vii

Interior maps used under license from © Shutterstock.com

Author photo courtesy of © Panos Skoulidas

ISBN: Print 978-1-64152-878-8 | eBook 978-1-64152-879-5

RQ

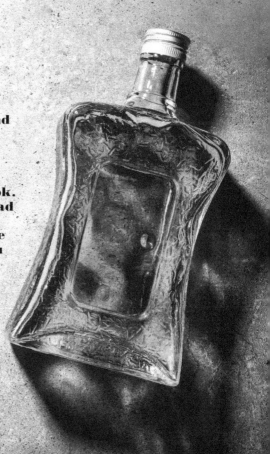

to my

**parents, Richard and
Carrie Green.**

**Thank you for your
support while
I worked on this book.
This was a tough road
at times, but your
support made all the
difference. I love you
both so much.**

CONTENTS

INTRODUCTION

WELCOME TO the *Beginner's Guide to Whiskey: Traditions, Types & Tastes of the Ultimate Spirit.* My name is Sam Green, and I've been enjoying whiskey for what seems like decades, but in actuality is only six years. You see, at the time of publishing, I'm just 27 years old. Nevertheless, in the six years since I've begun enjoying alcohol, my passion and respect for the brown nectar known as whiskey have grown exponentially. I've actually loved the idea of whiskey since I was in high school. Cigars and Scotch always seemed cool to me, though I really (really!) didn't start drinking until I turned 21, at which time I began to pillage my cousin Gary's selection. My mission became to grow my knowledge as quickly as my passion.

In pursuit of this quest, I began to research the work of coopers, the folks that make the barrels in which whiskey is aged; (master) distillers; and brand ambassadors. My thirst for knowledge, and for whiskey, continued to be insatiable. At 24, I became the first person in Southern California to become a certified Whiskey Sommelier. I achieved this by taking a master class, completed over two days, with an exam at the end. And still, my excitement to continue learning more about this nectar keeps growing, as does my love for the passionate community surrounding it.

By writing this book, my goal is to share my zeal by teaching you as much or as little as you want to learn about whiskey. We will cover regions of production, laws surrounding production, flavors, myths, tasting, glasses, and some favorite cocktail recipes. We will delve into individual categories, such as bourbon, rye, American single malt, Irish, Scotch, and Japanese whiskies. Of course, a book on whiskey would be incomplete without a brief foray into whiskey's role in history. We'll probe the Prohibition era in the US and the effect it had on the global whiskey market. We'll explore the origins and history of Japanese whiskey. And we'll dive into barrels used for aging whiskey. Have you ever wondered why whiskey is sometimes spelled without the "e"? Wonder no more. We'll cover that too.

This book caters to those of you who are just embarking upon your whiskey journeys. In fact, it is perfectly okay to read this book knowing nothing about whiskey except that you're interested in it.

But because the book runs the whole gamut, from history to tasting notes, my hope is that seasoned drinkers too will glean new information and advice from these pages.

So please allow me to guide you in developing your nosing and tasting habits while presenting you with the knowledge you need about the drink you are enjoying. The more you know about whiskey and the better you understand its origins and complexities, the more you will enjoy drinking it, keeping in mind that personal taste is ultimately the most important factor.

CHAPTER 1

the history of whiskey

Whiskey has been around for several centuries now, with a history going back as far as the 11th century. Throughout its lengthy past, whiskey has been used as both a medicine and a libation. For many years, doctors would prescribe whiskey for a variety of ailments. During the 13 years of Prohibition in the US, a prescription for whiskey, Cognac, or brandy was one of the only legal ways to get alcohol (the other legal loophole was ceremonial wine for religious purposes). Still, bootlegging, rum-running, smuggling, and home distillation all flourished.

The Original Spirit of Whiskey

One of the highlights of whiskey is its versatility. While its primary historical use was medicinal, in more recent centuries and up until today, it is a relaxing adult beverage that is treasured, celebrated, and enjoyed by seasoned and new drinkers alike.

For years, monks had been distilling neutral spirits from grapes. The term "neutral spirits" refers to neutral alcohol, such as vodka. It is distilled to such a high proof that there is essentially no flavor left. Upon moving to Scotland and Ireland from Rome between the years 1000 and 1200 CE, they began to distill what would become known as whiskey: a spirit distilled from grain, not grape, because grain was more readily available. Once King Henry VIII of England dissolved the monasteries in the mid-16th century, various medical professionals began to distill whiskey, along with individual former monks who continued the craft.

During this period, "whiskey" was not aged, at least not intentionally, and it certainly was not bottled. It was typically served out of a barrel and likely stored in pots or some other type of vessel. People would purchase it from the local pharmacist and then imbibe the "medication" as prescribed at home.

THE WATER OF LIFE

Whiskey, whisky, *uisce beatha* (pronounced Ush-Kuh Bah), *uisge beatha*, or even *aqua vitae*. What's the difference? Simply put, nothing other than the origin of the word, and the language of the country from where the spirit comes. *Uisce beatha* is the Irish Gaelic phrase for "water of life," while *uisge beatha* (with a "g," not a "c") is the Scottish Gaelic phrase.

What does the Latin phrase *aqua vitae* mean? You guessed it: Water of life. Over the years however, as Latin and Gaelic have fallen out of fashion and English has become one of the dominant languages spoken worldwide, the two Gaelic variations of water of life have evolved into the word we know today: whiskey.

A Changing Thirsty World

During the American Revolutionary War, a whiskey tax was levied to help pay off debts to foreign governments. Alexander Hamilton, Secretary of the Treasury, encouraged the federal government to take over the responsibility for paying the debt from the states. He instituted a policy where the big whiskey distillers paid six cents per gallon of whiskey sold, and the smaller distillers had to pay nine cents per gallon.

This policy did not last for long, because the taxpayers refused to pay in what became known as the Whiskey Rebellion of 1794. Excise officers were threatened. Things got violent and people got hurt. Sometimes, it escalated to the point of tax collectors being tarred and feathered! The violence continued until then-President George Washington sent a militia to quell the rebellion; the tax stayed in place until Thomas Jefferson repealed it in 1801.

Around this same time, in the late 18th century, the Industrial Revolution (and accompanying improvements to steam power and the steam engine) led to a more efficient distillation process. Using indirect steam to heat a still, versus the old method of direct coal fire, allowed for a more even heat dispersion. Today, the still is heated

with boiling oil or natural gas, which affords an
even steadier temperature so that distillation can
be consistent.

Prohibition & World War II

What exactly was Prohibition? Prohibition is the
colloquial name for the 1919 law that made the consumption, sale, transport, and import of alcoholic
beverages illegal, with the exception of medicinal
use. Formally, prohibition became codified as
the 18th Amendment to the US Constitution and
the law implementing prohibition was called the
Volstead Act.

Prohibition went into effect in 1920 and somehow
lasted 13 years, despite the widespread existence of
illegal alcohol across the country. The idea gained
momentum in the late 1800s when organizations
like the Women's Christian Temperance Union and
the Anti-Saloon League began grassroots campaigns
to ban the sale and consumption of alcohol. These
organizations believed that many societal woes
would be cured by a mandatory abstinence. And
Congress agreed, signing into law the 1919 Volstead
Act (over President Woodrow Wilson's veto), which
banned alcohol with the exception of religious wine
and medicinal consumption. It also left it up to each

individual state to enforce the law and define the rules for personal consumption.

In response to this new law, alcohol dove underground, and criminal gangs took over import, production, and sale. Bootlegging thrived as gangs smuggled liquor into towns and cities to be distributed through back alleys and speakeasies. The concept of the speakeasy—a secret room or bar, with admittance by password only—sprang up during this period.

Illegal distilleries and even backwood stills sprang up around the country. Back then, if someone ordered a glass of whiskey in a speakeasy, it was entirely possible that they were handed a neutral spirit (such as vodka) with flavor and color coming from who knows where. In fact, homemade concoctions blinded and killed a number of people during this period.

By the time of Prohibition's repeal, there really was no whiskey industry at all in America; Prohibition had brought it to a halt. What's more, Ireland and Scotland had lost their biggest market when Americans were no longer able to purchase or drink alcohol.

The whiskey industry in America took a further hit during World War II, despite Prohibition being a thing of the past. During the war, distilleries were repurposed to produce high-proof neutral spirits. At this time, distilleries were again forbidden from producing drinking alcohol; these spirits were used to make ammunition and rubber.

Survival & Revival

December 5, 1933 has become known amongst whiskey enthusiasts and liquor brands as Repeal Day. It was on that day that the federal government ratified the 21st Amendment to the Constitution, repealing Prohibition and making alcohol creation, distribution, and consumption legal once again. One of the major reasons for repealing Prohibition was the lack of enforceability. To this day, despite it being legal federally, there are still some places in the United States that opt to prohibit alcohol. These so-called "dry" counties and towns include places like Lynchburg, Tennessee where, despite housing a famous distillery, visitors are not allowed to drink.

Where did whiskey stand at the end of Prohibition? Fake "whiskey" (neutral grain alcohol flavored and colored to taste and resemble whiskey) had literally left a bad taste in the mouths of many people during Prohibition, driving them to other spirits and cocktails post repeal. Vodka was easily accessible and made for great cocktails because of its tastelessness. It mixed well, and got imbibers drunk. Whiskey was struggling, especially compared to its popularity before Prohibition.

Prior to Prohibition, Irish whiskey was hugely popular in the United States. America was one of the biggest markets. But when Prohibition went into effect, import and sale of Irish whiskey took such a dive that it put many distilleries out of business. It took until the late 20th century for the popularity of Irish whiskey to return, and now there are more Irish whiskey brands than in the past. Even some of the big names that once closed have been resurrected and are producing and successfully selling Irish whiskey once again.

Today, whiskey has reemerged as one of the most popular spirits in the world, with a constant influx of new brands. This influx is made possible because of what are referred to as "NDPs," or non-distilling producers. A brand will purchase whiskey from a distillery (if American, often out of Indiana; if Canadian, often out of Calgary), bottle it, and sell it as its own.

Major whiskey festivals the world over sell out year after year, both reflecting and contributing to whiskey's popularity. Everyone from beginners to well-known whiskey experts attend these festivals, and sometimes the experts will even work closely with a brand, helping to pour the product. Major companies spend thousands of dollars building elaborate booths or hiring promotional models to pour whiskey for the guests. Many times, smaller, local brands are regulated to the corners with humble, unobtrusive displays staffed by the distillery team and even local fans. Shows range from your local whiskey club doing a mini-fest in an airport ballroom, to national touring events that cost hundreds, sometimes thousands, to attend. (I've attended WhiskyFest, The Nth, and Whiskey and Barrel Nite just to name a few; all good shows with massive turnouts.)

The whiskey world is about more than the drink; it's about the community. I keep going back not just because I have the opportunity to try not-yet-released creations, but because I catch up with so many friends over a taste of whiskey. The excitement is contagious as I approach a booth where the distiller or brand ambassador will excitedly tell me that I need to try something. One of my favorite things was to see my late friend and mentor, Dave Pickerell, a master distiller and the man behind a good number of the popular brands on the market today. When he was at a show, he was the star, valued for his charm, knowledge, experience, and kindness. Though Dave was certainly unique, I have found that the whiskey community is made up of people who appreciate friendship, craftsmanship, innovation, and not least of all, a good dram shared.

CHAPTER 2

putting whiskey on the map

Is this glass of bourbon a whiskey? What about this glass of Scotch? Simply put, yes; those are both forms of whiskey. Whiskey is the umbrella term, and underneath that umbrella are variants, including Scotch, bourbon, rye, single malt, Irish, Japanese, Indian, Swedish, and even Tasmanian! It is a truly international product, and each country has its own unique take on the whiskey-making process, resulting in a variety of flavors.

Who Are the Big Five?

"The Big Five" in the world of whiskey are the five most known whiskey-producing countries: Scotland, Ireland, America, Canada, and Japan.

In America we have a several different whiskey styles, but America is home to bourbon, a whiskey distilled from a recipe (also known as a mash bill) of 51 percent or more of corn. Scotland is the birthplace of Scotch whisky. Canada is home to Canadian whisky (though they call everything in Canada rye), and Irish whiskey hails from, you guessed it, Ireland! And of course, Japanese whisky comes from Japan.

Rye is another common type of American whiskey, different from bourbon in that 51 percent rye grain takes the place of the 51 percent corn. American single malt contains 100 percent malted barley and comes from just one distillery (the rule is the same for single malt Scotch).

- **Scotland** is home to Scotch whisky. Note the lack of an "e" in the word "whiskey" here. It is not a hard and fast rule, but assume if there is no "e" in the name of the country, there is no "e" in that country's spelling of the word whiskey. Scotland produces five distinct categories: Blended Scotch, blended malt Scotch, blended grain Scotch, single malt Scotch, and single grain Scotch. A blended Scotch combines malted barley and malted cereal grains from at least one distillery. Blended malt or blended grain is a blend of either malted barley or malted cereal grains from at least two distilleries. Single malt and single grain Scotches are 100 percent malted barley or cereal grains from one distillery.
- **Ireland** produces its own variants of whiskey. The country makes single pot, single malt, blended, and single grain varieties.
- **Japan** is home to Japanese whisky. At the time of writing, the laws for Japanese whisky are still very lax. As a result, a percentage of Japanese whisky is actually Scotch whisky imported then bottled in Japan. There is still a fair bit of controversy surrounding Japanese rice whiskies because currently, of the big five, only America considers rice a distillation grain.

- **Canada** produces all sorts of different whisky variations, including but not limited to 100 percent rye whisky, and "rye" whisky that actually contains little to no rye (which is contrary to American laws, where the mash bill must contain a minimum of 51 percent rye to be considered a rye whiskey). In addition, Canadian whisky brands can add coloring and flavoring, which explains offerings that market themselves as peach, cinnamon, maple, or apple-flavored. Not all Canadian whiskies add these components.

INDIAN WHISKY

Contrary to popular belief, the country that consumes the most whiskey in the entire world isn't America or Scotland, but India. India is the largest consumer of whiskey in the entire world, with single malt being the fastest growing category. Additionally, India is a massive producer of spirits labeled as whiskey. But why isn't India in the big five? The answer is simple. The majority of Indian spirits are not actual whiskey, but are instead neutral spirit made from sugar cane or molasses with additives like imported malt whiskey or artificial coloring and flavoring.

Whiskey Worldwide

In addition to the big five mentioned above, many other countries produce whiskey. Australia, Sweden, India, Taiwan, and Kenya are producing whiskey! The biggest similarity between the countries you know and those you don't is their single malt production. Nearly all whiskey-producing countries have a distillery producing single malt, and they all follow the same laws: It must contain 100 percent malted barley, from one distillery. Some examples include Wales, which produces Penderyn; Australia, who make Starward; and some Taiwanese whisky brands, which come from the Kavalan Distillery.

All About Appellation

Does whiskey, like wine, have appellations? Well, yes it does, but before we even get into that, we need to touch on what an appellation is. The short answer is that an appellation is a protected region of land where the product (usually referring to wine) must be made.

While nowhere near as prevalent as in wine, it is becoming increasingly common to find a whiskey that sources all of its grains and water from the local area surrounding the distillery. In fact, distillers take pride in using everything local. In some cases, such as in Texas, if you're not making everything from grain to glass in Texas, you cannot be considered a certified Texas whiskey.

But there are also the more obvious occurrences of appellation in the whiskey realm. Anything labeled "Kentucky bourbon" can only be made in Kentucky, and, as you may recall, bourbon itself can only be made in America (including American territories like Puerto Rico). Scotch can only be made in Scotland. In a twist, Japanese whisky can technically be made anywhere, as long as it's bottled in Japan.

The Influence of Terroir

Terroir, the natural environment in which whiskey is produced, may not sound like a big deal, but it has a major effect on the flavor of the liquid in your glass. In Kentucky, for instance, distillers use a specific type of water available in the region that contains limestone, because of the rich minerality it lends to the taste. For peated whiskies like Scotch, the origin of the peat (which is used in the malting process; more on this on page 25) makes a significant difference in taste. The peat differs by climate. If it is from the island of Islay (pronounced Eye-luh) then you can expect it to be much brinier, more along the lines of burnt rubber and a campfire. If the peat comes from the northern isle of Orkney, then it tends to be much more heathery and mellow. Orkney, on the northern tip of Scotland, has very few trees and boasts a very windy climate. Islay is further south and endures less wind. The peat from both islands possesses an oceanic influence.

In fact, one of the major aspects of terroir to take into account is general climate. For example, if the climate has rapid and frequent temperature swings, aging whiskey will mature at a faster rate by entering in and out of the barrel staves more frequently and may have an older taste to it, even if it isn't an old whiskey. Specifically, the temperature changes cause the barrels to expand and contract, forcing the whiskey in and out, which is what creates the aging effect. All of that being said, the effects of terroir have not been 100 percent espoused by the world of whiskey and may not be for a long time to come. Nevertheless, I firmly believe that terroir does influence whiskey.

CHAPTER 3

how whiskey is made:

grains, malting, mashing & fermentation

The process of making whiskey can get quite complicated, so we will break it down into parts here. Some of the fun of enjoying whiskey is understanding and appreciating how it's made. This chapter will cover the types of grains producers can use, as well as the malting, mashing, and fermentation processes. In the next chapter, we will talk about distillation, maturation, blending, and bottling.

It's All About the Grain

Grain is the most important part of the whiskey-making process. Without a grain recipe (mash bill) you cannot make whiskey. To recap, the mash bill is the recipe that the distillery will mill, (sometimes) malt, ferment, cook, and distill.

Most whiskey is made from corn, rye, wheat, or barley, but those aren't the only grains that can be used. A distillery can use rice as the main grain or as the non-primary grain. There are whiskies on the market distilled from oat, millet, and even beer. Yes, some distilleries are taking that local craft IPA and distilling it into a whiskey.

Most distilleries do not harvest their own grain; they rely on a grain supplier/manufacturer to harvest, clean the grains of anything like soil, rocks, or other unwanted contaminants, and bag the grains before sending them to the distillery. When the distillery is ready to use the grain, it has often already been milled and is ready for the malting and fermentation processes.

Let's discuss the mash bill or the recipe of grains that the distillery then ferments and distills to make your whiskey. Specifically, the "mash" is the cooked grains and the "bill" is the recipe. For instance, "95/5" is a common mash bill used to make bourbon; this means the mix is 95 percent corn or rye and 5 percent malted barley. Not all distilleries have their own unique mash bill, particularly when it comes to single malt, where they are using 100 percent malted barley. In that case, each distillery may use different barley than the competitors, but it's a similar recipe.

There are two stages when I like to taste the product:

1. The mash as it's fermenting.
2. The new-make spirit (affectionately referred to as "white dog") after it has been distilled.

It is my philosophy, and I'm sure many others will agree, that if the new-make spirit isn't good, no amount of aging or finishing can fix and cover that up.

WHISKEY PRODUCTION

STEP 1:
Growing of the grain
(rye, wheat, barley, corn, oat, millet, etc.)

STEP 2:
Harvest and clean off debris

STEP 3:
Malting
(when applicable)

STEP 4:
Mashing

STEP 5:
Fermentation

STEP 6:
Distillation

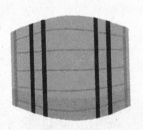

STEP 7:
Aging
(when applicable)

STEP 8:
Blending, proofing,
and bottling

Malting

Malting is the process of germinating the grains to allow the mashing process to extract sugars from inside the grain. The process allows the sugars that are trapped inside the husk to be converted and accessed. Malting lends a flavor to the whiskey akin to a malted beverage.

The grain recipe or mash bill doesn't always have to be malted, especially if barley is not the primary grain. In some cases, producers can skip right to the fermentation process if they don't need to extract extra sugars.

Barley, however, needs to be "woken up" through the malting process. It entails soaking the barley in water for a few days to let the unfermentable starches convert into fermentable sugars. To stop the malting process, producers will dry the grain.

In Scotch whisky most people assume that the burning of peat halts the malting process, but that's not always the case. Peat renders a certain smoky characteristic to the barley that many distillers and blenders do not want, so those producers will dry the barley in a kiln. This is often done with steam or hot air.

Many of the distilleries that use malted grains use the "traditional" style of floor malting. Floor malting entails soaking the barley, letting it begin to germinate, and then laying it out on a cool floor in a specific warehouse. Distillers then shovel and rake it by hand to allow air to enter the grain, because a lack of oxygen means dead barley.

Peat

What exactly *is* peat? Essentially, peat is baby coal that comes from a type of moss called Sphagnum, and is formed in bogs. Peated whiskey is whiskey in which the grain is dried (at least in part) by peat. It is used as a fuel source to dry the grain and gives the whiskey that smoky, rubbery, burnt tire smell and flavor that so many people love.

Much like coal is formed over thousands of years under pressure inside the earth, peat is formed in a similar matter. It's decayed plant matter, found in bogs and swampy climates. While most associate peat with Scotland and Scotch whisky, it can be found globally and it varies from region to region. For instance, peat that is found in the Scottish Highlands will be much more mellow than peat found on Islay. Peat from Ireland has its own unique flavor profiles and characteristics compared to peat that may be found in North America. The peat in North America is found primarily in Canada and the northern United States.

Why did they start using peat in Scotch? Before there were steam-powered kilns to dry the barley and halt the germination process, distillers used peat because it was what they had available.

Mashing

Mashing is the next stage in making all types of whiskey. First, distillers separate the grain from any rocks and dirt that may have been left behind from harvest (milling). The distillery then takes the malted (or not) grains and puts them into a mash tun, which is essentially a giant kettle or pressure cooker, often made out of copper and very nice to look at. The mash tun uses heat and water to extract the fermentable sugars from the grains by breaking them down. The yeast eats the sugars, and then transforms them into ethanol and releases carbon dioxide. The result of mashing is a low-alcohol substance called wort, which is then fermented with the addition of yeast and nicknamed "distillers' beer."

The Importance of Water

Whiskey contains water. A lot of it. It may not make a lot of sense, and you may be saying "But it's alcohol! It's whiskey!" Yes, but unless it's 100 percent abv (alcohol by volume), it is still composed, at least partially, of water.

If there is water in your whiskey, how did it get there? The answer isn't quite so simple, because nearly every stage of the whiskey-making process uses water in one way or another. You obviously need water to grow the grains. You also need it when you're malting the grains. As mentioned above, malting grains entails steeping them in water until they just barely begin to germinate, then cutting that process off. You need to add the grains to water to begin the mashing process.

The type of water also makes a difference because of the minerality. For instance, in Kentucky, most (if not all) brands use limestone water. One reason is that if there is iron left in the water when you make the whiskey it will turn black—and the limestone filters out iron. No one wants inky, black whiskey. In addition to filtering out the iron, the limestone water also adds some minerals such as calcium to the whiskey.

But limestone water is specific to Kentucky bourbon. What about the rest of the country? Some minerals in the fermentation process are good, and even encouraged. They help the yeast reproduce and create the flavors that are unique to each distillery. Minerals in the water are one of the reasons no two distilleries produce whiskey that tastes identical, even if they're doing everything else the same.

Fermentation

Now we're getting to the fun part. I have a theory: If your mash is good, then your white dog will be good. If your white dog is good, then your whiskey will be good. So far, I've yet to be proven wrong. If you have a local whiskey distillery nearby, I highly recommend going for a tour and asking to taste their mash while its fermenting.

Fermentation is the creation of the distillers' beer. Yeast eats the sugars to create alcohol. Different yeast strains eat at different rates. And different distilleries have different lengths and methods of fermentation. Some ferment for a few days, others for longer. The length of time a distiller ferments depends on its yeast strain and on whether or not it will lose or gain more flavor. A lengthier fermentation may also yield a higher alcohol content, which will affect flavor as well.

Some distillers do open air fermentation, which allows the carbon dioxide to escape and the air from the environment where the washback is stored to come in contact with the wort. Others do closed fermentation, where they will allow the carbon dioxide to escape, but won't allow the outside air to come in contact with the wort.

The yeast eats the fermentable sugars in the wort and creates carbon dioxide and alcohol. This allows the wort to be distilled, because it has created enough alcohol for a distillers' beer, but not enough alcohol for a whiskey.

In fermentation, if a tank is "open face" you can see the wort fermenting and bubbling. That's the carbon dioxide rising to the surface, and despite what it may appear, it is usually not very hot. Most distilleries will allow you to taste it. Generally speaking, the mash tastes yeasty, grainy, and sweet, but in the best way possible.

Washbacks

What is a washback and why does it matter? A washback is the vessel in which distillers ferment mash. The two common types are oak and stainless steel. Some people believe that a wooden washback imparts more flavor to the wort and can potentially add more flavor to the whiskey. Others note that it is more difficult to clean the wooden ones after use than it is to clean the stainless steel washbacks. Still others argue that it is unnecessary to wash the washbacks because of the presence of beneficial yeast enzymes in the wood from previous fermentations.

Yeast and Flavor

Yeast plays a prime role in the creation of whiskey and each whiskey's unique flavor profile. Put very simply, it eats the sugars created by the mashing of the grains and turns them into alcohol ready to be distilled. Many distilleries even have their own proprietary yeast strain that they keep under lock and key. Yeast is a necessary ingredient for any whiskey; in fact, yeast, along with wood, is a major contributor to each whiskey's unique flavor. For example, suppose next-door neighbors Distillery A and Distillery B are both using new charred French oak barrels, but they each use their own proprietary yeast. Despite experiencing the same climate, the whiskey they produce will be vastly different.

Other factors that weigh on the flavor of a whiskey include the height of the barrel warehouses, the fill level on the barrels, the temperature the yeast can withstand, the rate at which the yeast eats the sugars, and even the way the barrels are coopered (the term for making barrels).

Patience Is Key

Time is one of the major facets to creating a decent-tasting whiskey. Sometimes it's ready earlier than expected, but if you lay down a barrel of whiskey tomorrow, don't expect it to be ready for a good few years.

While the fermentation process certainly takes time, it is the aging process that tests patience the most. A distiller may hope that a whiskey will be ready at a certain age, or certain date, and can bottle it whenever they want. But generally, to really pick up a great deal of depth of character, rich aromas, and deep flavors, the whiskey needs time to age in that barrel. It's not ready until it's ready.

CHAPTER 4

how whiskey is made:
distillation, aging, blending & bottling

In the last chapter we learned the first steps to making whiskey. We went over the mash bill, milling, malting, and fermenting. In this chapter, we'll discuss the back half of the whiskey making process: distilling, aging, blending, proofing, and bottling. We'll go into cask types, why almost all whiskies are blends, and much more. This part of whiskey production can get a bit technical, so we'll take it one step at a time.

Distillation

Distillation is a complicated process involving low wines, high wines, heads, hearts, and tails cuts. In its simplest form, distillation entails taking fermented mash (distillers' beer) and pumping it into a copper still.

Here is a basic, step-by-step account of the distillation process:

1. To begin distillation, distillers pump their wash/distillers' beer into a *wash still*.
2. They heat the wash to a boil, which separates the alcohol from the water because the alcohol has a lower boiling point.
3. The alcohol then turns into a vapor and travels through what is called the *lyne arm*, which is at the top of the still and leads to the condenser. Note that the bigger the still and/or the higher the lyne arm, the more delicate the whiskey will be because the heavier flavor molecules (esters and fatty acids) aren't able to travel far. A shorter, squatter pot still will lead to a heavier, creamier spirit, while a taller still will produce a lighter more delicate spirit (though a taller still can produce a heavier spirit depending on the amount of reflux).

4. The alcohol enters the condenser from the lyne arm. The condenser has cold water constantly running through it to cool it and allow the alcohol vapor to condense and be turned back into a liquid.

5. The first distillation run is now complete and has produced what is called a *low wine*. Low wines do not contain enough alcohol by volume to be whiskey.

6. Next, distillers transfer the low wine to the *spirit still*, where it is distilled a second time to a much higher proof. It is at this point that the distiller will start taking "cuts." That is when they switch the output location of the spirit coming off the still.

7. The first cut the distiller makes is what is known as the *heads* or *foreshots*; this cut contains very volatile compounds that are unsafe for consumption. The heads are taken and put into a holding tank first.

8. The second cut is known as the *hearts* or *middle cut*. This is what will ultimately end up getting barreled to age.

9. This second cut comes off of the still at a much higher proof, usually around 140 to 160 proof. After distillers make this cut, they direct it into the *spirit safe*, a type of storage container. Often, they will leave a small cut of the *tails*, also known

as *feints*, in the hearts cut for flavor. The tails are the ends of distillation; they hold some flavor compounds.

10. Once the second cut has been made and redirected into a spirit safe, the distiller will keep the still heated and distilling until the spirit remaining in the still reaches an alcohol content of around one percent. This is to ensure that they are not wasting any residual alcohol that may be left in the still if they were to stop the distillation process.

The question is, how do distillers know when to make the cuts? Well, distillation is both an art and a science, and presents no easy task. Part of the job of the distiller is to know what temperature the still must be heated to, how long that takes, and at what temperature to get to what part of the cut.

Stills

There are two common but distinct kinds of stills used in whiskey distillation: the copper pot still and the column still. The column still is also known as the Coffey still, named after Aeneas Coffey, the Irish excise officer who patented the design. There are benefits to both types of stills. The pot still is used for batch distillation, while the column still is used for continuous distillation. Think of distilling on a pot still like making something by hand. Distillation on a column still is much more consistent. It distills by using metal plates that run the length of it on the inside, and each time a spirit passes over a plate, it gets re-distilled.

The importance of the still extends beyond just the scientific aspects of distillation into superstition as well. It is a common belief in certain distilleries that any dent or ding on the still affects the flavor of the distillate. Distilleries will even go so far as to replicate the exact dents and dings when they have to get a new still, because they feel it affects the process and the distillate that much.

Distillation Speed

Low and slow, hot and quick, or even hot and slow—the speed of distillation makes a difference in terms of the quantity of contact the distillate has with the still. Contact with the copper is really important because it removes unwanted flavors, like those produced by sulfur. Copper is a reactive metal and those unwanted flavor molecules will get trapped inside of the still instead of in the whiskey. This process technically also involves the amount of reflux of the tails compounds and still height. Springbank, for example, has a long and slow distillation speed but has a much heavier spirit, meaning there was less reflux.

Spirit Safe

A spirit safe is a metal and glass box, often locked, into which most distillers direct the spirit. Once the spirit comes off the still and through the condenser, it passes into the spirit safe where it is then redirected, depending on what cut they are distilling at that time. If it's the heads or foreshots, it is transferred to one storage tank where it is held to be

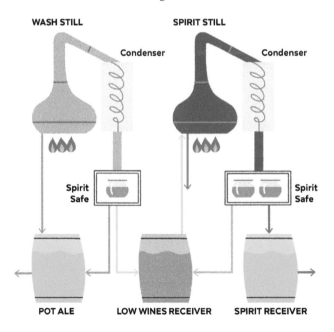

WASH STILL · Condenser

SPIRIT STILL · Condenser

Spirit Safe

Spirit Safe

POT ALE · LOW WINES RECEIVER · SPIRIT RECEIVER

redistilled later or discarded. If it is the hearts cut, it is transferred to a different tank where it will wait until it is barreled.

Historically, the spirit safe was a tool of the tax collector. Its purpose was to prevent the distiller from sampling their own product and therefore taking money from the government. After all, they were being taxed on the volume they distilled, not what was left in the barrel after maturation. Presently, the spirit safe is used as a way to measure alcohol content, using a device called a hydrometer. A hydrometer measures how dense the new-make spirit is. The distiller will compare the density measure to a chart to check the alcohol by volume.

Aging

The maturation of whiskey, or aging, is perhaps my favorite part of the whiskey-making process. There is a lot of information to break down. Before we get into the nerdy stuff, though, let's start with a bit of history.

Whiskey is aged in wooden barrels for historical reasons. It used to be that whiskey wasn't bottled to be sold; rather, it was sold to the "retailer" (bar, corner store, pharmacy) in a barrel. Retailers would sell the whiskey to customers directly from that barrel. The customers could then store it in a clay pot or a glass bottle of their own.

Each whiskey-producing country has its own laws and rules for the creation of whiskey. Trade agreements allow for the import of whiskey into other countries as long as it complies with the laws of the country of origin. There are, however, a few common rules and regulations that cross country lines. All whiskey must be aged in oak barrels (sometimes called casks), except in Canada, where other types of wood are permitted. Whiskey cannot be aged in stainless steel or glass. All whiskey must be bottled at no less than 40 percent alcohol by volume. And all countries have a proof limit (though the exact number varies) over which whiskey cannot be distilled. Each country has its own laws on the minimum time whiskey must age. Bourbon, for instance, just has to touch a barrel. Scotch and Irish whiskies must be barrel-aged a minimum of three years.

Aging is a major factor in a whiskey's flavor and color. Here's how it works. The new-make spirit is moved from a stainless steel holding tank into wood barrels. (In larger distilleries this is done by an automated process, while in smaller distilleries it is often done by hand.) Once filled, those barrels are set aside to let the whiskey age and mature. The barrel isn't airtight and it's not waterproof either. It's held together by pressure and force from the hoops around it. As the temperature changes, the barrel will swell and shrink, forcing the whiskey in and out of the wood. Over time, this is what gives whiskey its color and a large portion of its flavor (the rest coming from the mash bill and distillation processes). Evaporation is a part of the maturation process as well. As much as 2 percent of the spirit, called the angel's share, is lost from every barrel.

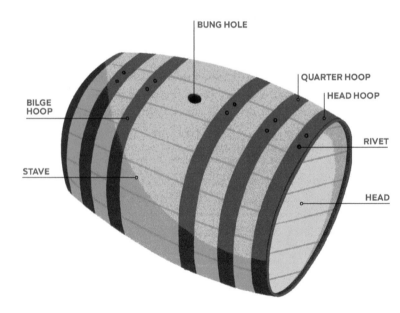

BUNG HOLE

QUARTER HOOP

HEAD HOOP

BILGE HOOP

RIVET

STAVE

HEAD

BARREL SIZE AND FLAVOR

Why do some distilleries use 50-liter barrels and others 200 liters? Big-name whiskies are experimenting with using smaller barrels too. Whiskies aged in smaller barrels will often mature faster because the smaller surface area allows for much more contact between the new-make spirit and the wood of the barrel. Although many of these small-barrel whiskies are good, you can't rush Mother Nature. Smaller barrel whiskies may lack the subtlety and nuances that come from time spent maturing in a larger barrel.

Charring

Before it was common to age whiskey, barrels were used as storage containers for anything and everything: Raw fish, rusted screws, oil, etc. When whiskey makers began to use barrels, they charred the interior of used barrels in order to remove contaminants, sterilize them, and make them safe to store something for consumption.

Now the charring is an essential part of the aging process. Today, there are four general levels of char, each with a varying length of time on the flame. There is no industry standard for char levels. Some companies, like Michter's or Koval, use a toasting method with their barrels, in which the barrels are lightly toasted but not charred. Charred oak barrels are the most common. Charring caramelizes the wood sugars and literally chars the barrel itself.

- **Level 1** is a light char. It's basically a step above toast. In this case, there is less char for the whiskey to go through to get into the wood tannins and sugars of the barrel. This means that there will be less char flavor after maturation and less caramelization.
- **Level 2** is a medium-light char.
- **Level 3** is a medium char. This is one of the most common char levels for American whiskey. It will

impart a nice woodiness to the whiskey, as well as heavier notes of vanilla and caramel.

- **Level 4** is the heaviest char possible. It's also referred to as an "alligator char," because the inside of the barrel looks like scaly alligator skin. This char level breaks down the barrel the most and imparts very heavy oak and smoky char notes.

Breathing

When temperatures rise, whiskey barrels swell, forcing the whiskey into the wood of the barrel. When temperatures drop, barrels contract, forcing the whiskey out. This expanding and contracting is known as breathing. But what does it mean when we say that the whiskey is being forced into or out of the barrel? Picture a barrel that is not assembled; the wood pieces that make it up are called staves. Each barrel stave is wood that has been cut, cured, dried, and then assembled into a barrel. The tightness or looseness of the wood grain determines the porousness of the wood. The more porous the wood, the more the new-make spirit will be able to penetrate into the barrel when it swells.

Warehousing

Whiskey is generally stored in one of two types of facilities. The first is a rickhouse, which is commonly made of wood, metal, or brick and can store barrels up to eight or twelve high; the second is a dunnage warehouse, generally used in Scotland. Dunnage warehouses are built with stone walls and a bare earthen floor, so the temperature won't fluctuate as much. The benefit of the rickhouse lies in the construction of it. The higher the rickhouse, the more barrels a producer can store. The barrels at the top will be hotter and will have more water evaporation due to that heat. Less water equals higher proof spirits. The lower floors are the opposite, with less water evaporation. Different rickhouses are made out of different materials. Some are stone, others tin, and others still are made out of wood. Each building material will influence how the temperature affects the barrels aging inside, especially in Kentucky, where there are major temperature swings on a daily basis.

Another important factor regarding warehousing is where and how barrels are stored in the warehouses. Some blenders and distillers feel that there are "sweet spots" for aging while others disagree. But what they all will agree on is that no two barrels are alike. A barrel from Warehouse A on floor 4 may have a lot more pepper notes than one from Warehouse D on floor 8. There is not currently a way to predict what a barrel will taste like in the future based on what spot in the warehouse it is in. Blenders and distillers work together tasting samples almost daily to determine when a whiskey is ready or, in some cases, if it is exceptional enough to be a single barrel release.

Blending

When people talk about blended whiskies, they're usually referring to Scotch, and even then, they're thinking of cheap or low-end blends that are considered "rot gut." But what not all whiskey drinkers realize is that almost all whiskies are blends. Unless a bottle of whiskey says "single barrel" or "single cask," it's a blend of multiple barrels. The reason producers mix whiskey from multiple barrels is so that they create a consistent flavor across the board from batch to batch and year to year. They mix together all of the differences from the different barrels to create one consistent flavor and texture.

If a bottle does say single barrel, or single cask, it means that that batch of whiskey came from one individual barrel. It will have a similar but slightly different flavor from the main batch.

Bottling

After the whiskey barrels have been dumped, blended, and proofed, it is time to bottle. A brief note on proofing first: This step is when the distiller will add water to bring the alcohol by volume (abv) down to bottling strength. A whiskey must be a minimum of 40 percent abv or 80 proof. Water can also be added to achieve barreling strength. When first distilled, the spirit has a very high abv (this could easily be over 70 percent but for most whiskey it's not more than 80 percent, or 160 proof), and distillers cannot legally barrel whiskey at that high of a proof.

Similar to the barreling stage, the whiskey is first transferred to a holding tank. Depending on the distillery, bottles will go onto either an automatic or manual assembly line. The whiskey then fills the bottles of various sizes. The United States is the only country that has its own special bottle size, 750 milliliters, as compared to the rest of the world's 700 milliliters. A specialized machine fills several bottles at a time to the same fill level, ensuring consistency. Then the cork is placed on the bottle and a plastic, foil, or wax seal is applied before packing it for shipment.

CHAPTER 5

scotch

Don't let its size deceive you; this small country, Scotland, is one of the biggest producers of whiskey in the entire world. While mostly on the mainland, distilleries exist on almost all of the islands as well. Islay, Skye, Orkney, Jura, and Raasay are just a few of the Scotch producing areas. When most people think of Scotch, they may think of peaty, smoky flavors. While these flavors are common from Islay distilleries, mainland distilleries present other flavor profiles as well. In this chapter we will explore the different types and tastes of Scotch whisky.

SCOTLAND

What Is Scotch?

What is Scotch? The short answer is that Scotch is a category of whiskey produced in Scotland. But of course, that's not a very *good* answer. The laws regulating Scotch whisky are monitored by the Scotch Whisky Association, not to be confused with the private members club of a similar name. The SWA, founded in April of 1942, originally created the rules for Scotch whisky in 1988, then updated them in

2009. The basic laws state that in order for Scotch to be Scotch it must be fermented and distilled in Scotland; it must be aged for a minimum of three years in oak barrels; it cannot be bottled at less than 40 percent alcohol by volume; and it must be distilled at less than 190 proof. Scotland's climate, which is cold and wet, causes its whisky to mature more slowly.

Types of Scotch

At the time of publication, there are 128 (legal) Scotch whisky distilleries that can produce Scotch, within six specified regions of Scotland: Highland, Speyside, Islay (Eye-luh), Islands, Campbeltown, and the Lowlands.

Within the umbrella category of Scotch, there are five subcategories. These include single malt Scotch, single grain Scotch, blended Scotch whisky, blended malt Scotch, and blended grain Scotch. The most popular Scotch whiskies are blended Scotch followed by single malt. Names like Johnnie Walker, The Macallan, The Glenlivet, Chivas Regal, and Monkey Shoulder are well-known, massive sellers.

Let's break down these different types of Scotch:
Single malt Scotch is Scotch whisky that is fermented, distilled, and aged at one distillery in

Scotland for a minimum of three years. It is made out of 100 percent malted barley and can have no additives except for water and a small percentage of e150a, which is a caramel coloring designed for spirits. To be called "single malt Scotch," it must be distilled on a pot still.

A *single grain Scotch* is also distilled at one distillery, but is made from 100 percent malted cereal grains, which can include corn, rye, wheat, or barley. Single grain is almost identical to single malt, except that legally it is allowed to be distilled on a column still.

Blended Scotch whisky, like its name describes, is a marriage of multiple Scotches. It is a blend of malt and grain whiskies, typically (but not necessarily) coming from multiple distilleries.

Blended malt and *blended grain Scotch* whiskies fall under similar laws for their make. To be a blended malt, you must be a blend of at least two single malts from at least two distilleries. A blended grain must be a blend of at least two single grain Scotch whiskies from at least two distilleries.

THE FINISHING TOUCH

When it comes to Scotch (or whiskey in general) what does it mean to "finish" it? To finish a scotch, or any whiskey, is to transfer it into a second barrel for a final, short-term maturation. Usually this "finishing" process lasts for about six months. Scotch is commonly transferred from ex-bourbon casks (the primary type of oak barrels that Scotch ages in) into sherry wine casks. Several producers use Sauternes (a sweet French wine) casks, and some even use brandy, port, or Cognac casks! The finishing process will impart flavors associated with the barrel type into the whiskey, and this is the only legal manner to "flavor" your Scotch (or any whiskey other than Canadian, but we'll cover that in chapter 8). If not done correctly, the finish can result in poorly flavored whiskey that is unbalanced, oversweet, oaky, or just unpleasant.

The Taste of Scotch

The six regions of Scotland all produce whisky with different flavor profiles.

Islay, probably the most famous of Scotland's whisky-producing islands, is known for producing whiskies that have bold notes of ash, tar, iodine, rubber, and tire fires. Whisky made on Islay is almost always peated, with the exception of the Bruichladdich (Brook-lad-ee) core range and a few Bunnahabhain (Boo-nuh-ha-vin) expressions. If you're a fan of smoke, Islay whisky is a good choice.

Whiskies from Speyside commonly have a lot more fruit and raisin notes. They will be sweeter and more delicate on the tongue. These Scotches are rarely peated.

The whiskies from the Highlands, while similar in flavor to those coming from Speyside, give off bolder flavors. You'll taste rich dark fruits, cocoa, and sweets like pies and cookies. The Highlands have more peated Scotch then any region except for Islay.

In the Campbeltown region of Scotland, distilleries often produce a much heavier-tasting whisky. The Scotch here is a very full bodied, robust, and powerful malt that gives a lot of flavor and literally feels heavy. In this region, there is a good mix of peated and unpeated Scotch whisky, so make sure to check the bottle.

The Lowlands of Scotland are famous for producing a lot of the country's grain whiskies. Here you will find some single malt distilleries, but mostly single and blended grain distilleries. Grain whiskies tend to have a much lighter flavor profile, featuring ripe fruits, heavy influence from the barrel, and a fair bit of the grain shining through. They make a great introductory Scotch.

Last but not least are the other Scottish islands, including Skye, Orkney, Jura and Raasay, Arran, Lewis, and Mull. The Isle of Skye is home to the peated single malt Scotch whisky Talisker and the new Torabhaig (Tore-a-vague) distillery. On Arran you'll find the Arran distillery; the Isle of Lewis is home to Abhainn Dearg; and Orkney is home to Scapa and Highland Park. Jura produces Jura Scotch whisky. On Raasay sits a relative newcomer, the Isle of Raasay distillery, and on Mull, the Tobermory distillery produces Tobermory and Ledaig.

INEXPENSIVE	AFFORDABLE	EXPENSIVE
Monkey Shoulder – Fruity and malty	**Kilchoman Machir Bay –** Smoky and fruity	**Springbank 25 –** Rich, fruity, heavy
Glenlivet Founders Reserve – Corn, vanilla, oak, stone fruit	**Glenfarclas 12 –** Sherried, malty, balanced	**Bowmore 25 –** Delicate smoke, sweet sherry
Johnnie Walker Black Label – Touch of smoke, dried fruits	**Benromach 10 –** Notes of smoke, rich fruits, caramels and toffees	**Dalmore 18 –** Malty, stone fruit, dark chocolate

irish whiskey

Irish whiskey was one of the biggest exports out of Ireland, and one of the most popular categories of whiskey, until suddenly it wasn't. What changed? There are a number of factors that contributed to the decline of Irish whiskey, not the least of which was American Prohibition. Other factors included the rise of Scotch whisky and Scottish distillers' use of the column still (which increased Scotch production), patented by former Irish exciseman Aeneas Coffey; the Irish Civil War, which coincided with WWI; and the fighting between the British empire and the Irish government for control of Ireland.

After this "fall" of Irish whiskey, three of the main distilleries joined into one, the Midleton distillery. Fast forward to the early 21st century and Ireland is back to the whiskey producing powerhouse it was before.

IRELAND

Only Made in Ireland

There is just something about the way the Irish make their whiskey that draws people to it, especially novice drinkers. In fact, there are two particular brands of Irish whiskey more iconic than the rest. If you guessed Jameson (the top-selling Irish whiskey in the US) and Bushmills, you would be correct. Not only are they well known, but they are great starting points for enjoying Irish whiskey. What makes

Irish whiskey unique? By law, all Irish whiskey is a minimum of three years old. These whiskies are much lighter in body and are sometimes a lower proof, without sacrificing any flavor. Irish distillers achieve this balance because many, but not all, Irish whiskies are triple distilled. Distilling twice is more than adequate to get a high enough proof spirit to age into whiskey, but the addition of a third distillation creates a much lighter spirit, in both flavor and body. Irish whiskey tends to be more grain- and caramel-focused after it comes out of the barrel.

Irish blends, which popularized the triple distillation method, are the number one seller in the category of Irish whiskey. The interesting thing about Irish blends is that the grains aren't milled, mashed, fermented, and distilled together. Rather, they're blended together after maturation. Each grain component is distilled and aged; then, when they mature, the components are blended together and bottled.

Like most of the world, Ireland uses former bourbon barrels for their primary maturation, as well as a number of different barrels for finishes. A second truly unique characteristic of Irish whiskey production is its single pot still. Despite the widespread use of single pot still, Irish producers also make single malt, single grain, and blended Irish whiskies at the 28 legal distilleries in the country.

Drinks with Distinction

The most common production method of Irish whiskey is the single pot still. Irish single pot still is a style of whiskey made with malted *and* un-malted barley. In the late 1700s, the English government imposed a tax on malted barley rather than on the number of stills, so in order to circumvent that tax, the Irish distillers did two things: They added a third still, because if they were no longer being taxed on the number of stills, why not increase output capacity; and they added unmalted barley to their mash. The mash bill of their pot still whiskey became at least 30 percent malted barley, a minimum of 30 percent unmalted barely, and the remainder other cereals like corn, wheat, and rye.

Much like in the rest of the world, Irish single malt is distilled at a single distillery, and made from 100 percent malted barley. Primarily aged in ex-bourbon barrels, it can be finished in oak barrels. Sherry barrels are often chosen because of the current popularity of sherry cask-finished whiskies.

POITÍN

Poi-tin, poit-in, poi-shin? Pronounced pot-cheen, it's the Gaelic word for "small pot," and it was illegal until 1997. Poitín today is viewed as the white dog from a whiskey distillery, but it's actually Ireland's original native spirit. In fact, whiskey evolved in Ireland from Poitín. Poitín makers—generally farmers and others making small batches in their homes—looked around for material to distill. They settled on potatoes, apples, and wheat, among other resources.

Poitín became illegal in the 17th century in Ireland, because the producers were so decentralized and refused to adhere to the tax requirements. In 1997, it once again became legal to produce and consume Poitín in Ireland. It is becoming more popular and is served in more and more pubs because of its link to Irish heritage.

The Taste of Irish Whiskey

The flavor profile coming off of Irish whiskey is light, and even the single malts aren't particularly heavy distillates, so it is a great introduction to the world of whiskey as a whole. The flavors are a lot more approachable for an entry level whiskey drinker. The majority of Irish whiskey is either blended or single pot still. Generally speaking, because there is a higher cereal grain content in these whiskies, they are more grain forward and sweet, especially because of the triple distillation. The Irish single malt has more malt, vanilla, and oak characteristics.

INEXPENSIVE	AFFORDABLE	EXPENSIVE
Tullamore D.E.W. – Light, grain forward, malty	**Powers John's Lane** – Sherry cask, caramel, vanilla, toffee, butterscotch, pralines	**Midleton Very Rare** – Pepper, sweet corn, malt
The Sexton – Malt forward, sherry cask sweetness	**Bushmills Black Bush** – Malt forward, sherry, approachable	**Writers' Tears XO Cognac Finish** – Grain and malt, light caramel and burnt caramel, mellow crème brulee, medium spice/heat from abv, Red Delicious and Granny Smith apples
Jameson Original – Grainy, very light, oaky; vanilla and caramel essence	**Teeling Plantation Rum Finish** – Subtle rum-esque flavors, fruity, apple and pineapple. Some banana, sugary/molasses	**Bushmills Acacia Wood (Distillery exclusive)** – Robust body, saltwater taffy, saline, oaky, hints of baking spice, cardamom, bitter, syrupy

american whiskey

The category of American whiskey is very large and broad. While perhaps the best-known subcategory is bourbon, there is also rye, Tennessee whiskey, and other lesser-known types. This chapter centers on the big three, exploring flavor, rules, and myths. We will also briefly touch upon the blossoming category of American single malt whiskies, and how they are similar to their Scottish counterparts.

UNITED STATES
OF AMERICA

Bourbon

There are so many myths surrounding bourbon.
Let's dispel them up front. One of the most common
myths is that bourbon gets its name from Bourbon
County in the great state of Kentucky. While no one
really knows *for sure* where the name bourbon originated, it's thought to have come from Bourbon Street
in New Orleans, Louisiana.

Another pervasive myth is that all bourbon has
to be from Kentucky. Though most bourbon does
come from Kentucky (approximately 90 percent) the
reality is that bourbon merely has to be a product of

America. President Lyndon B. Johnson passed an act of Congress in 1964 codifying bourbon as America's official spirit.

Now that we have conquered the two biggest myths surrounding this spirit, let's dive into what makes bourbon bourbon. To be called bourbon, a spirit must comply with the ABCs of bourbon:

- **A**merican-Made – Bourbon can only be made in the United States of America and its territories.
- **B**arrel – Bourbon must be aged in a new charred oak barrel.
- **C**orn – Bourbon must be a mash bill of at least 51 percent corn. The other 49 percent can be anything a distiller chooses. Some of the other grains used are rye, wheat, oat, millet, and even quinoa.
- **D**istillation proof – In order to make bourbon, it cannot be distilled higher than a specific proof— in this case 160 proof, or 80 percent alcohol by volume.
- **E**ntry proof – The bourbon cannot go into the barrel any higher than 125 proof.
- **F**ill proof – Bourbon must be bottled at 80 proof or higher.

- **G**enuine – In order to be labeled as bourbon, it cannot have anything added to it pre- or post-barreling, except water.

The ABCs do not dictate how old bourbon must be to be legally called bourbon because there is no age minimum; it just needs to be aged, whether for one minute or one year. The only time age matters is when referencing straight bourbon. In order to be considered a straight bourbon, a distillery must follow all the rules outlined above for regular bourbon, but must also age the bourbon for a minimum of two years. If it is aged less than four years, the distiller must state the age on the bottle.

The bottle must bear the age of the youngest whiskey in the blend (remember, unless it says single barrel, all whiskey is a blend). If a distiller has four-year-old bourbon blended with twelve-year-old bourbon, the bottle will state that it is four years old.

Bottled in Bond

Bottled in Bond, or BiB, is a bourbon and rye regulation that stipulates that bourbon or rye must be aged in a federally bonded warehouse. In addition, it must be aged a minimum of four years, and be bottled at exactly 100 proof. It must be distilled at one distillery, during one distilling season (January through June or July through December), by one distiller. The label must also identify it as a Bottled in Bond product and state the distillery name. Bottled in Bond bourbon originated in in the late 1890s as a response to the production of fake and/or adulterated bourbon. It serves as an extra certification of authenticity for bourbon brands, but earning BiB certification is optional. BiB bourbons are interesting because of their single distillation season origin, rather than the more common practice of blending various barrels from various seasons.

Limestone Water

As we discussed earlier, the limestone water is how many of the Kentucky distillers account for the unique flavor of their bourbon. One contribution of the limestone is that it adds minerals to the water. Limestone water is also high in calcium content, which, according to Kentucky distillers, is a tremendous positive when it interfaces with the yeast.

But limestone water is not a necessary component to bourbon. There is some fantastic bourbon being made elsewhere in the US without the use of limestone water. So, the jury is out as to whether limestone actually makes a difference in bourbon.

Some non-Kentucky (non-limestone) bourbons include: High West, Belle Meade, King's County, and Balcones.

The Taste of Bourbon

The beauty of bourbon is that the corn gives it a sweet taste. But so many other factors have an influence on the flavor as well: the mash bill, yeast strain, where it is aging (temperature-controlled versus non-temperature controlled rickhouses), and if barrels are rotated or not. Some distilleries rotate their barrels, and it tends to lend a more even flavor profile to the whiskey laying rest inside.

Notes of sweet corn, vanilla, caramel, oak, and toffee are all very common in bourbon. Other common flavors include chocolate and baking spices like clove, cinnamon, and cardamom. But here's the biggest thing, and I cannot stress this enough; when tasting whiskey, there is no wrong answer to what flavor you may be picking up, because everyone's palate is unique.

INEXPENSIVE	AFFORDABLE	EXPENSIVE
Wild Turkey 101 – Rye forward, bready	**Henry McKenna 10 Year Bottled in Bond** – Sweet, spicy, oak, vanilla, caramel	**Booker's 30th Anniversary** – Spicy, sweet, corn heavy
Maker's Mark – Sweet, wheat, corn	**Woodford Reserve Double Oak** – Oaky, corn heavy, char, sweet, malty	**Elijah Craig 18** – Oaky, corn heavy
Jim Beam Black – Corn forward, slight oak notes, sweet	**High West American Prairie** – Rye forward, sweet, corny, vanilla, caramel, toffee	**Clyde May's 10 Year Cask Strength Straight Bourbon** – Sweet corn, savory, peppery, hot, oaky, caramel, powerful, smooth

CAUTION AGAINST A DISTILLER'S NIGHTMARE

In July of 2019, Jim Beam had a warehouse catch on fire, causing the company to lose around 45,000 barrels of young whiskey. The year before, the Barton Distillery, home of 1792 Bourbon, had a partial warehouse collapse. It is not known exactly how many barrels fell, but it was estimated at around 9,000. Thankfully, the distilling community in Kentucky is fairly close knit, and even though they are competitors, distilleries will often help each other in times of crisis. Because of recent issues like these, the Kentucky Distillers' Association (KDA) has devised a checklist to protect against future incidents.

The Taste of Tennessee Whiskey

When people hear "Tennessee whiskey," they often think of two things: Strawberry wine or Jack Daniel's. What is it about Tennessee whiskey that makes it different from other types of American whiskey? The answer is something called the Lincoln County Process, which we will explore below. Other basics include the fact that Tennessee whiskey has to be made in Tennessee and must follow all the laws of bourbon. Tennessee whiskey is a small category within the broader category of American whiskey, but it is slowly growing.

Typically, the flavors of Tennessee whiskies are very similar to bourbon, because the only real difference is the contact with charcoal. In my experience, Tennessee whiskey does tend to be drier and sweeter than bourbon. In 2017, author and historian Fawn Weaver created the Tennessee whiskey brand Uncle Nearest (by contracting with a Tennessee distillery), in honor of the slave Nathan "Nearest" Green, who taught Jasper Newton "Jack" Daniel how to make whiskey.

The Lincoln County Process

Besides being distilled in Tennessee and following the bourbon laws, in order to be legally considered a Tennessee whiskey, a new-make spirit must go through the Lincoln County Process (LCP). The LCP dictates that the new-make spirit must touch charcoal before barreling. Jack Daniel's, for example, filters its new make through 10 feet of sugar maple charcoal, drip by drip, before barreling it. The Dickel distillery fills a vat of charcoal with new-make spirit and then drains it all out at once.

In the 1950s, the federal government tried to tell Jack Daniel's that its whiskey had to be called a bourbon. The company argued that because of the LCP, the whiskey it was making tasted much different than other bourbon and that the charcoal mellowing/filtration changed the structural makeup of the whiskey in the bottle/glass/barrel. The federal government agreed and Jack Daniel's won the case.

There are actually several whiskey distilleries in Tennessee that are making delicious bourbon. Because they don't go through the LCP, however, they can't legally be called Tennessee whiskey.

INEXPENSIVE	AFFORDABLE	EXPENSIVE
Jack Daniel's Old No. 7 – Sweet, corn forward, candy	**Uncle Nearest 1856 –** Very bourbon-esque	**Jack Daniel's Sinatra Select –** Oaky, vanilla, corn heavy, semi-sweet
George Dickel Old No. 8 – Sweet, bourbon-y, oaky	**George Dickel BiB –** Heavy molasses, toffee, corn, oak	**George Dickel No. 12 –** Oaky, caramel
Uncle Nearest 1884 – Sweet, oaky	**Jack Daniel's Gentleman Jack –** Oaky, sweet, robust	**Jack Gold No. 27 –** Maple forward, corn, candied sweetness

Rye Whiskey

Although it is not as popular, rye whiskey is actually like bourbon's older brother. It possesses a more robust flavor, with spicier notes rather than the sweeter ones prevalent in the corn in bourbon. Unlike bourbon, distillers can make rye whiskey anywhere in the world. Canada is famous for it, and in Scotland several producers have rye whiskey aging in barrels right now while they argue with the Scotch Whisky Association on what they can and cannot bottle.

Rye whiskey in America must adhere to a very strict set of laws, which are nearly identical to the laws of bourbon. The major difference between the regulations for bourbon and those for rye whiskey is that rye must have a minimum of 51 percent rye in the mash bill instead of 51 percent corn. Other than that difference, the rules are exactly the same, even for Bottled in Bond rye.

The Taste of Rye

Rye is a spicier grain and therefore does not have as broad appeal. It is a bolder, more robust, more intense grain, but the whiskies that it produces can be fantastic.

INEXPENSIVE	AFFORDABLE	EXPENSIVE
Rittenhouse BiB – Some spice and oak, approachable, somewhat sweet	**Minor Case Sherry Cask Rye –** Vegetal, spicy, sweet raising	**Booker's Rye –** Spicy, oak forward
Sazerac Rye – Young and spicy, but sweet	**Limousin Rye –** Sweet, dry, approachable	**Willett Family Estate –** Spicy, sweet, oaky
Woodford Reserve Rye – Sweet, oaky, toasted caramel	**Russell's Reserve 6 Year –** Spicy, sweet, oaky	**Hochstader's Family Reserve 16 Year –** Sweet, oaky, spicy

American Single Malt

Let's touch on one of the newer categories of American whiskey: American single malt. It's a burgeoning category of whiskey that is widely misunderstood. While everyone is drinking bourbons and ryes, American single malt is being left on the shelves or mistaken for Scotch whisky. So, what *is* American single malt? It is not yet an actual legal category of American whiskey, but the American Single Malt Whiskey Commission, while pursuing legal whiskey status for American single malt, has established a standard of identity for it. The standards state that in order to be American single malt whiskey, it must be:

- Made from 100 percent malted barley.
- Distilled at one distillery.
- Mashed, distilled, and matured in the United States.
- Matured in oak casks not exceeding 700 liters.
- Distilled no higher than 160 proof.
- Bottled at 80 proof or higher.

American single malt is similar in flavor to Scottish or Irish single malt, because they all use 100 percent malted barley, but the environment in which they are aged differs. American single malt may be a touch "creamier" in the mouthfeel.

INEXPENSIVE	AFFORDABLE	EXPENSIVE
Hudson Single Malt – Vanilla, malt forward, toffee, butterscotch	**FEW American Single Malt –** Sweet, balanced, oaky, toffee	**St. George Baller –** Fruity, malty, rich, slightly creamy
Colkegan – Mesquite, malty, subtle caramel, toffee	**Balcones "1" Texas Single Malt –** Sweet, malty, oaky, vanilla, creamy	**Stranahan's Diamond Peak –** Vanilla, oak, caramel, cocoa
Stranahan's Regular – Sweet, slightly loose/watery, approachable	**Westward –** Malt forward, cocoa, dark chocolate	**Westland Garryana –** Peppery, sweet, rich cocoa

canadian whisky

When you think of Canadian whisky, it's quite likely you'll think of one brand: Crown Royal. This is not a surprise, because the company sold enough whisky to fill just under 26-and-a-half Olympic-sized swimming pools in 2018, according to *The Spirits Business*, a well-respected media outlet for the drinks industry. Despite the popularity of Crown Royal, there are several other fantastic brands coming out of Canada. These brands produce single malt, rye, and, yes, even a few flavored whiskies. Some American distilleries are even sourcing spirits from Canada. The majority of Canadian whisky is blended and Canada uses a unique whisky-making process. In this chapter, we'll "nerd out" on Canadian whisky.

CANADA

Defining Canadian Whisky

To define Canadian whisky there are several factors
to consider. One notable difference between
Canadian and other whiskies is that, in Canada,
distillers can legally add flavoring and coloring, up to
9.09 percent of the overall blend. In my experience,
a lot of the high-quality whisky never makes it out of
Canada, or at least never makes into the US Either
the Canadian distillers are too small to export or

the American requirement that all bottles be at least 750 milliliters (while most of the rest of the world uses 700 milliliters) is too onerous. In order to export to the US, distillers from other countries must alter their bottle size per American regulations. The laws for Canadian whisky are quite clear. Distillers must:

- Use cereal grains. These include, corn, wheat, rye, and barley, among a few others.
- Ferment the grains in Canada.
- Distill the whisky in Canada (in any manner: column, pot, single distillation, double distillation, etc.).
- Age the whisky in Canada, using a wooden cask no larger than 700 liters (the cask must be wooden but not necessarily oak).
- Age for a minimum of three years.
- Ensure a minimum of 40 percent alcohol by volume in the bottle.
- Make sure that a maximum of 9.09 percent of the blend is non-whisky (coloring or flavoring).

Whisky Streams

In Canada, there are two streams of whisky being produced: regular whisky and flavored whisky. Canada is legally allowed to export whisky with flavoring and/or coloring added into the blend. This allows for popular whisky brands on the market to contain cinnamon, peach, maple, or apple flavors. In other countries, like America, adding flavor would render it no longer a legal whiskey. It would become more along the lines of a liqueur, which generally has a lower alcohol by volume. But in Canada this is a completely legal and profitable way to sell whisky. When I first started drinking whiskey, I was not able to handle it well, but when my father went out and picked up a bottle of maple-flavored Canadian whisky, I began to see what the fuss was about. It became one of my entry points into the world of whiskey.

Only in Canada

Because Canadian distillers are able to use different types of wood to make barrels, it presents opportunities for unique flavors and textures. Canadians use many other types of wood aside from oak (although they do use oak as well) to age their whiskies, including chestnut, redwood, and walnut. They even sometimes use oak barrels that in other countries would no longer be good, such as oak that is close to being neutral, meaning it has previously been used three or more times. Each type of wood will impart a different flavor.

Canadian whisky producers are permitted to age their spirits in a wooden cask of 700 liters (185 gallons) or less, while most other countries often do not exceed 200 liters (53 gallons) for primary maturation. This allows for bigger batches, and fewer overall warehouse space requirements. But it also means that the aging whisky will have less contact with the barrel.

9.09 PERCENT RULE

The 9.09 percent rule is a law in Canada that allows distillers to add up to 9.09 percent of non-whisky to the final blend before bottling, while still legally calling it whisky. Canadians can even add caramel coloring to the whisky to make it appear older than it actually is. They use flavor to make it richer or to reach a different market internationally, with offerings like salted caramel whisky.

There is absolutely nothing wrong with flavored whiskies, and if you enjoy them, that's great! Some flavored whiskies are put to great use in cocktails. I enjoyed a cinnamon whisky cocktail at a party recently and it was fantastic. I've even baked with cinnamon whisky.

The Taste of Canada

The biggest Canadian distilleries resemble factories more than anything else because of the massive amount of Canadian whisky they produce. There are fewer distilleries in Canada that cater to the entire demand. The major brands have production in regions such as Alberta, Manitoba, and Ontario. In 2018, Canadian whisky distillation returned to Montreal upon completed refurbishments to the Old Montreal Distillery.

Another well-known name in the Canadian spirits industry (aside from Crown Royal) is blender Dr. Don Livermore. At a distillery in Windsor, Canada, Dr. Livermore and the distillers make gin, rum, vodka, liqueurs, Canadian whisky, American whiskey, and other spirits for numerous companies located in and out of Canada.

In Calgary, Alberta Distillers Limited produces whisky for companies that choose not to, or are unable to, have a distilling component to their process. This distillery is the Canadian counterpart to a similar American one in Indiana. In fact, most of the whisky made in this Calgary distillery actually leaves the country, rather than being bottled and going on shelves in Canada. The twist is that some of the brands that the Calgary distillery supplies will then ship the final product back to Canada to sell there.

INEXPENSIVE	AFFORDABLE	EXPENSIVE
Crown Royal – Sweet, vanilla, slight oak	**Pike Creek –** Rye, vanilla, oaky, sweet port	**J.P. Wiser's 18 –** Oaky, nutty, vanilla, toffee
J.P. Wiser's Rye – Oaky, silky, vanilla, toffee pudding, rye spice	**Crown Royal Blenders' Mash (Bourbon Mash) –** Oaky, sweet corn, spicy, toffee and caramel	**Lot No. 40 –** Sweet, rye spice, oaky
Canadian Club – Peppery, caramel, oak, rye	**Caribou Crossing –** Oak, rye, vanilla	**Crown Royal Monarch 75th Anniversary Blend –** Peppery, sweet, vanilla, toffee, caramel, bread, rye

japanese whisky

The Land of the Rising Sun is home to one of the most sought-after categories of whisky, Japanese whisky. In fact, bottles of Japanese whisky can be so popular that the liquor stores can't keep them on the shelves. They are so coveted that there are whole subsections of the whisky community that only want bottles of Japanese whisky. Why are they so coveted? Unfortunately, there is a shortage of real Japanese whisky in the world. But what does it mean to be "real" Japanese whisky? That's a complicated question with a complicated answer, which we will dig into in this chapter.

JAPAN

All the Difference

Masataka Taketsuru is widely regarded as the father of Japanese whisky. He was a chemist and business-man who brought whisky distillation to Japan in the early 1920s. Jokichi Takamine was actually the first person to be mentioned on the record with the words "Japanese" and "whisky" in the same sen-tence in an 1892 *Chicago Daily Tribune* article. The paper discussed Takamine's process of fermenting corn with koji (a fungus used to ferment soybeans) for a higher yield. To be clear, this was not Japanese whisky, but rather a Japanese gentleman's approach at making whiskey in America using a Japanese fermentation process.

Compared to the rest of the world, Japanese whisky has not been around for long. Before bringing whisky to Japan, Taketsuru studied the whisky-making process in Scotland from 1918–1920. During that time, he studied organic chemistry at the University of Scotland and apprenticed at several distilleries to get hands-on experience.

The first commercial distillery in Japan was the Yamazaki distillery, established by Shinjiro Torii and Taketsuru in 1923. Originally, Torii and other distillers imported whiskies from Scotland, blended them with Japanese distillate, and bottled them in Japan.

This practice has continued to this day, with several Japanese whisky brands blending single malt or blended Scotch with Japanese whisky or using Scotch entirely in lieu of any Japanese distillate. Some of the unique characteristics of Japanese whisky include that some Japanese distillers ferment with koji when they use rice as the grain, and they use a fermentation process called parallel dual fermentation.

Fermenting with Koji

We mentioned koji being used to ferment corn, but how does that work? Simply stated, koji is a fungus that helps convert starches in the grain (in this case, rice) so that the yeast can more easily digest the fermentable sugars. This process is used in the production of shochu, a Japanese liquor made from rice and occasionally aged; baijiu, Chinese rice spirit; Haku Vodka; and Japanese rice whisky. It was also used in the process of making bourbon by Takamine in America. According to Japanese whisky expert Chris Uhde, koji produces a cleaner fermentation, because in addition to converting the starches in rice into fermentable sugars, it also removes unwanted materials like methanol.

The Japanese use a unique fermentation technique called parallel-dual fermentation. While they are fermenting with koji, they are also doing a more common fermentation with distillers' yeast. This dual method results in a more delicate but distinct spirit with unique flavors.

While Japan is not the only country to ferment with koji, it is the primary country to produce rice whiskies. Just as a note, there are also several distilleries producing rice whiskey in America, but according to *Whisky Advocate,* these distilleries are not fermenting with koji; they're actually producing in the styles of other Southeast Asian spirits, such as baijiu or shochu.

Mizunara Oak

In our discussion of oak so far in this book, we have been referring mostly to two types: Quercus Alba (American oak) and Quercus Robur (English or European oak). When it comes to Japanese whisky, the more relevant species is Quercus Mongolica—specifically the subspecies Crispula (Mongolian oak, better known in the whiskey world as Mizunara oak).

Mizunara oak is a type of tree that is native to Japan, China, and several other Asian countries. It is the "hot" oak right now, meaning every whiskey maker wants to age whiskey in it. The flavor it imparts is unique and highly sought after. But there are numerous hurdles to overcome in order to use it. First, Mizunara is very hard to cooper or make into barrels, because unlike American or European oak, Mizunara trees tend to bend, twist, and knot instead of growing perfectly straight. This is partly due to the fact that they often grow on the sides of mountains.

The second challenge with Mizunara oak is the grain of the wood. It has a very open, very porous grain structure and therefore the barrels made from it tend to leak, which ends up yielding costly losses in product in the barrel warehouse. A third issue with Mizunara is that the trees need to be around 200 years old before they can be cut down and turned into barrels, and because of this, there are very few barrels made each year (less than 500).

There are some absolutely fantastic whiskies finished in Mizunara. Note that I said "finished." This is because it is usually not financially feasible to do full term maturation in Mizunara oak, due to the leakage mentioned above. There are several distilleries that have released full-term Mizunara-aged Japanese whiskies, however. The Suntory distillery has released an 18-year-old Yamazaki single malt aged exclusively in Mizunara barrels. At the time of print, the 2017 release is selling for almost $3,000 (if you can even find it). In addition, the Kurayoshi Distillery has released a NAS (non-age stated) Matsui single malt aged fully in Mizunara. When available, this retails for around $100.

The taste of Mizunara oak is a difficult one to describe because the affordable whiskies that use it usually only do a finish of a few months (I would estimate no more than six). My opinion here is that Japanese whisky aged in Mizunara gives off banana, tropical fruit, pineapple, and lychee notes, but not always. And because Mizunara is a natural material, the level of toast or char can add or remove flavors.

Northern versus Southern Maturation

Why does Japanese whisky mature at a faster rate in the south of Japan than in the north? The answer is climate. Northern Japan is a lot more consistent in its temperatures and colder than the south, so the barrels stored there expand and contract less. As we discussed earlier, this means less moving in and out of the wood, which leads to a slower rate of flavor development. This is not a negative, because it resembles the low and slow distillation method and the whisky is likely to develop deeper, richer flavors. Southern Japanese whisky matures more quickly because of the vast temperature swings common to the region, not dissimilar to a bourbon aging in Kentucky. Expect more barrel influence in a shorter time period. Japanese whisky does not have a minimum age requirement, though most are at least three to five years old.

AWARD-WINNING WHISKY

As I write this, Japanese whisky is a hot commodity. Part of its elevated status is attributable to the many awards it has won over the past several years. At the 2019 World Whiskies Awards, Japanese whisky took home several of the "world's best" honors. Hibiki 21 Year Old won World's Best Blended; Ichiro's Malt and Grain won World's Best Blended Whiskey Limited Edition; and Nikka Taketsuru 25 Year Old took an award for World's Best Blended Malt.

Are awards a significant statement on the quality of whiskey? The answer is open to interpretation. I view awards as a benchmark for the whiskey industry and for the whiskey drinker. They let the distillers and ambassadors know that they're on the right track and that the products they're putting out are being enjoyed. But I do find it unfortunate, as do other drinkers and aficionados, that

when a particular whiskey wins an award, its price will skyrocket in bars, restaurants, and liquor stores. Generally though, awards have their place as a guide for the whiskey drinker to find something new, and for the whiskey company to know they're producing something people like.

The Taste of Japanese Whisky

At the time of publication, there are 20 to 25 active Japanese whisky licenses, and several shochu distilleries producing rice spirit and selling it in America as Japanese whisky. This number is bound to change within the next two years, as I expect to see more shochu brands selling in America as rice whisky, as well as an increase in whisky licenses. The top three Japanese whisky producers are Suntory (Yamazaki, Hakashu, Hibiki), Nikka (Coffey Malt, Coffey Grain, Yoichi, Taketsuru), and Mars (Akashi, Iwai, Chichibu, Ichiro).

The challenge with Japanese whisky is defining it. The current Japanese laws and regulations pertaining to its production and sale are quite vague.

They require merely that it be made from malted grains and bottled in Japan. That's it! As discussed on page 87, you can import Scotch, bottle it in Japan, and then sell it as Japanese whisky. There is some controversy over Japanese producers using the black koji method to make rice spirit, and then selling it in America as whisky. Japanese rice whisky is only considered to be actual whisky in countries *other than* Japan. Japanese laws require that Japanese whisky be made from malted grains. I usually identify Japanese whisky by looking for the taste of Fuji or Red Delicious apples.

INEXPENSIVE	AFFORDABLE	EXPENSIVE
Suntory Toki – Light, sweet, malty	**Mars Iwai –** Fruity, malty, subtle oak notes	**Hakushu 12 –** Smoky, floral, sweet
Nikka from the Barrel – Sweet, spicy, vanilla, caramel, fruity	**Matsui Mizunara Cask –** Chocolatey, malty, pineapple, tropical	**Akkeshi Peated –** Smoky, briny, malty, fruity
Akashi White Oak – Light, balanced, sweet, floral	**Nikka Coffey Malt –** Floral, malt forward, vanilla	**Taketsuru Pure Malt 17 –** Smoky, floral, Fuji apples

craft whiskey

No doubt if you have searched for whiskey in a liquor store recently you've seen a fair number of whiskey brands that you have never heard of. They might say "craft," "small batch," "handcrafted," or some combination of similar buzz words. But what does any of that really mean? What makes this "handcrafted" bottle of two-year-old straight rye whiskey from Rhode Island worth $50 while a four-year-old bottle from Kentucky is $25? In a word: marketing. Sure, that two-year-old whiskey might be good, but it might also be terrible. That's the thing about the craft whiskey movement; it is sometimes defined by trend and style rather than by actual quality. There is no currently existing legal definition of small batch or handcrafted whiskey. But that is not to say that the movement is without merit or great whiskey.

The History of Modern Craft Whiskey

The late Dave Pickerell was one of the biggest pioneers of the craft whiskey boom. Pickerell was the former master distiller for the well-known wheated bourbon brand Maker's Mark from 1994 until 2008, when he left to start his own company.

Pickerell became best known by whiskey enthusiasts for being one of the founders, the master distiller, and public face of WhistlePig Whiskey. While Pickerell was probably the most well-known face of the modern craft spirits movement during his lifetime, he was definitely not the only one. Other notable names include Chip Tate, one of the original founders of Balcones Whisky in Texas, and Jorg Rupf, founder of St. George Spirits in Alameda, California.

Defining Craft Whiskey

We can call craft whiskey a marketing term, but that's not completely fair, nor is it the whole story. There are some fantastic whiskey brands that produce on a smaller scale, that are craft in the true sense of the word. The definition of craft is a gray area, however, because in the US there are no legal guidelines for qualification. Nothing exists beyond common sense definitions of terms like "small batch" and a few trade organizations (like the American Distilling Institute) putting out their own unenforceable guidelines. In fact, the American government does not discern between large- or small-scale distilleries. Generally speaking, a craft whiskey maker will produce a smaller amount of product in a given year than a large-scale brand. Oftentimes, these craft whiskey brands will have more rigorous production standards and will be more hands-on in the process of making their whiskey from start to finish. Because of the lack of rules regarding these craft whiskies, the concept of "small batch" can vary widely, as can the meaning behind "handcrafted." When comparing a company like Garrison Brothers making a small batch, to a larger company like Beam Suntory making a small batch whiskey like Booker's Bourbon, the term can mean two entirely different things. Booker's, being a branch of a bigger brand, will produce more whiskey for their small batch than Garrison. There is no definition for what is considered to be "small batch."

Now let's take a look at the term "handcrafted." When it says "handcrafted" on a bottle label, one would naturally assume that the whiskey inside is grain to glass: harvested, mashed, milled, distilled, bottled, and then labeled by hand. And while often the whiskey *is* made that way, it doesn't legally have to be in order to use the term "handcrafted" on the label. There is no legal definition or federal enforcement of the term at all. That means that companies can say something is handcrafted and they don't have to prove it.

The Challenge of Independence

New whiskey brands, especially craft brands, face many hurdles on their route to market. Let's start with the most obvious one: capital. It takes a lot of money to start a whiskey brand. Even if a new brand is purchasing whiskey from another distillery to bottle as their own, it's still thousands of dollars for the barrels alone. There are also all the legal fees associated with starting any company, as well as the additional step of getting approval by the government.

Another massive hurdle that any whiskey company faces is time (which is also financially costly). Whiskey takes time to age and mature. To combat this issue, some companies scientifically accelerate the age of their products. For instance, Lost Spirits Distillery in downtown Los Angeles uses UV to mimic the chemical structure of a 23-year-old spirit in just six days. But this option is cost prohibitive to many new companies. If a distiller is aging whiskey in the traditional manner, it takes years before it's ready.

So how do they make money in the meantime? Some distillers sell vodka, gin, or other clear spirits that don't require years of aging before going to market. But for small, independent distillers, they may not have the financial wherewithal to withstand the time requirements.

Previously, I mentioned purchasing whiskey in bulk from an existing distillery and then selling it under a new label. This may be a good option for a smaller whiskey brand just getting its start. In fact, it's a common practice; there is no shame in being a non-distilling producer (NDP) as long as the brand is forthcoming about that fact. Midwest Grain Products, better known as MGP, is a distiller located in Lawrenceburg, Indiana that produces whiskey for hundreds of whiskey brands. This is a very common practice in the industry, especially for new brands. There are two ways to purchase whiskey if a brand is not distilling it itself. Sourcing is often associated with purchasing a preexisting whiskey or mash bill. Contract distilling is a subset of sourcing in which the brand tells the distillery what the mashbill or recipe it wants to use is. Sourcing presents a great option for brands to get a start while they wait for their own whiskey stock to mature.

The Taste of Craft Whiskey

One of the wonders of whiskey is that no two brands will taste exactly the same. Even if they come from somewhere like MGP, with a semi-standardized mashbill, barrels are like snowflakes in that no two are identical. That's one reason why single cask whiskies are fun to taste and compare. The beauty of craft whiskey, aside from how individual and varied it is, is that producers have the luxury to be (1) more open to experimentation; and (2) interested in the feedback of customers. They often will try out different barrels, different mashbills, and different aging times. And while these craft brands are not necessarily going to bottle product based strictly on their customers suggestions, they often look for ways to connect with their customers and value customer feedback. Many brands have semi-personalized news-letters and will send an email or even a free gift for a birthday. The big names of the whiskey world are moving toward innovation and experimentation, but are still a few years behind some of the craft whiskey brands on the market today.

CHAPTER 11

how to drink and taste whiskey

If any chapter in this book is going to make you really want a dram, it will be this one. So, go to your home bar, grab your favorite whiskey-drinking glass, pour yourself your favorite whiskey, and dive in. This chapter will explore the nuances of whiskey tasting, including how to choose glassware, how best to nose the whiskey in your glass, and the most expert ways to taste whiskey. We will go over the choices of neat versus on the rocks, and explore some of my go-to whiskey cocktails. Keep in mind that the most important component of learning about, tasting, and drinking whiskey is that you honor your own preferences and enjoy the experience.

Glassware Matters

Or does it? The answer is that, while great glassware can improve your whiskey-drinking experience, it's not necessary. The bottom line is that there is no wrong glass for drinking whiskey. There are several glasses that are specifically designed and just right for the exact purpose, though, and they work great, so I encourage you to try them.

The most renowned of the whiskey nosing/tasting glasses is the Glencairn Glass, made by Glencairn Crystal in Glasgow, Scotland. It's the slightly tulip-shaped glass that whiskey bars throughout the world often use to serve their guests. Another glassware maker that is steadily growing in popularity is Denver & Liely (D&L). D&L offers a few different hand-blown glasses with unique shapes designed to accentuate the spirit inside. D&L offers glasses specifically designed for whisky, gin, agave spirits, and bourbon.

Why do these glasses work so well? The short answer is science and engineering. The longer answer is that they were designed with very specific parameters. The glasses are designed to concentrate the aromas of the spirit and to allow the lighter alcohol vapors to waft off. The Glencairn Glass boasts a patented design that captures the aroma in the base of the glass (the company calls it the bulb). From there, the neck of the glass forces it to travel upward and concentrates the aromatics of the whiskey. According to Glencairn, if you start on the outer rim of the glass and slowly move your way toward the center, you will detect different layers of the whiskey. Glencairn is the current industry standard glass for nosing and tasting. The company also offers a Canadian whisky glass, which is designed for use with Canadian whisky plus a mixer such as soda, or the addition of several small, or one large ice cube.

The D&L glass is a different shape than the Glencairn glass in that it has a wider base and simply tapers as it travels up. How does that affect the aromatics of the whiskey? According to Denver Cramer, one of the founders of Denver & Liely, the shape of the glass directs airflow control and delivery to the palate. The glasses are hand blown and designed to split the notes of the whiskey, separating the top layer of volatile alcohol vapors from the aromatics of the whiskey in the glass itself. This glass is unique in that it has a heating channel built into the glass so that if you wish to warm your whiskey through the heat of your hand, you can. The wider mouth of the glass allows for a better sip and lets the nose to be part of the tasting experience without being overwhelmed by the alcohol vapors.

When asked about their separate bourbon glass, which has a larger base, Cramer said it was designed to balance the sweetness of the corn-based spirit. Because bourbon tends to be a sweeter whiskey, D&L didn't want hands to warm the spirit, so they created this glass to improve the nosing and tasting of bourbon while separating the spirit from the heat of the hand.

Some believe that a stemmed glass is better for nosing and tasting because the hand isn't warming the spirit. There are whiskey connoisseurs on both sides of this debate. At the end of the day, what ultimately matters isn't whether or not you're using the right glass, but whether you're enjoying what's in the glass.

Nosing Whiskey

When nosing a glass of whiskey, the best practice is *not* to stick your nose right into the glass—at least not if it's a glass that concentrates the aromas. If you do, you'll be greeted by a huge waft of straight alcohol. You won't be able to smell much of anything and a large portion of the flavor of the whiskey will be muted as well.

So what is the best way to nose whiskey? Nosing whiskey, first of all, is very much what it sounds like; it involves taking in the aromatics of the spirit via your sense of smell to make sure you can smell the spirit in the glass. To do this, leave your lips slightly parted and breathe in through your mouth. A huge part of nosing whiskey is actually tasting it on your palate before even taking a sip. By inhaling through your mouth, you will be able to taste and smell some of the notes of the whiskey before it passes your lips.

Prepping the Taste Test

There are many ways to drink and enjoy whiskey. Neat, on the rocks (on ice), with a couple drops of water, or in a cocktail. I always tell people that the only wrong way to drink whiskey is the way that you don't enjoy. The way you drink whiskey has the potential to change the flavor profile of the whiskey in your glass, because you are diluting the alcohol content and releasing more flavor. No matter what your topic of discussion, there will always be groups of people who are "purists." In the case of whiskey, these people tell you that you shouldn't drink it on ice, with water, or in a cocktail. I disagree with the purists. You should drink whiskey in a way that is tailored exactly to your taste.

Neat

Drinking whiskey neat means enjoying it straight up, unadulterated, and without ice or water. This is my preferred method of drinking whiskey, because it simply tastes better to me this way; nothing is affecting the taste. That being said, drinking whiskey neat may not be for everyone. Those who are new to drinking whiskey may prefer to try it out on the rocks or with water first to get used to the flavor and experience before drinking it neat.

On the Rocks

When you order a glass of whiskey on the rocks, you generally get 1.5 ounces to 2 ounces of whiskey served over ice. The ice will chill the whiskey and dilute it at the same time, lowering the proof of the whiskey. The cold will also dampen and even mute some of the flavors of the whiskey. If you're going to enjoy whiskey on the rocks, use either a large cube or sphere, as those will melt slower and cause less dilution.

A Splash of Water

The great thing about adding a splash or a couple of drops of (flat) water to whiskey is that you will cut some of the alcohol by dilution, and also allow more flavors to come forward. Generally, I find that just a few drops of water (more may mellow the flavor) really helps to open up the whiskey. Especially with higher proof whiskies, the drops will make them easier to drink.

A common question when adding water to whiskey is what temperature to use. I prefer to use room temperature water, but if I only have cold water in front of me, that will do in a pinch. I tend to just dip my index finger into the water glass and let a drop or two of water fall into my whiskey; otherwise, I'll use an eyedropper and add about three to five drops. At a bar, order your whiskey neat with a water back and ask for a straw to use as a dropper.

Whiskey Cocktails

I love whiskey in cocktails. My go-to whiskey cocktail is a split-base daiquiri using overproof rum and a smoky Islay Scotch, like Laphroaig (see recipe below). There are three categories of cocktails:

- **Stirred** (where you add everything to a mixing glass and stir over ice). These are more spirit-forward. Two classics include the Old Fashioned (page 110) and the Manhattan (page 110).
- **Shaken** (where you add everything to a metal cocktail shaker and shake over ice). This category includes favorites like the Penicillin (page 111),

Split-Base Daiquiri (page 112), and Egg White Whiskey Sour (page 112). Shaken cocktails generally include the spirit, citrus, and a modifier.

- **Built in glass** (you make the cocktail in the glass in which it will be served). Probably the most well-known "built in glass" whiskey cocktail is an Irish coffee.

Below are recipes for some of my favorite whiskey drinks. The Old Fashioned, Manhattan, and Egg White Whiskey Sour are all classic cocktail recipes, the Split Daquiri is a modern riff on an old standard, and the Penicillin is a modern classic. Each of the cocktails listed here are fairly easy to make, with the exception of the Egg White Whiskey Sour, which is a bit more involved.

Old Fashioned

The classic cocktail's classic cocktail. The Old Fashioned is a staple cocktail on any whiskey bar menu. There are many riffs on this legendary cocktail, including the use of rum or mezcal.

YIELD: ONE SERVING

INGREDIENTS:

1.5 ounces bourbon (or rye)

0.5 ounce simple syrup (this is a 1:1 ratio of sugar and hot water)

4 dashes bitters (typically Angostura is used, but you can use any you choose)

INSTRUCTIONS:

Stir all ingredients over ice.

Pour over fresh ice in a rocks/old-fashioned glass.

Garnish with orange peel (lemon for rye) and serve.

Manhattan

Created at the Manhattan Club in New York City in the 1870s in honor of a then-presidential candidate, this cocktail has become another true classic.

YIELD: ONE SERVING

INGREDIENTS:

2 ounces bourbon (or rye)

1 ounce sweet vermouth

2 dashes bitters

INSTRUCTIONS:

Stir all ingredients over ice.

Pour into a coupe glass.

Garnish with cherry and serve.

Penicillin

A modern classic. Most people assume that this cocktail is from days gone by, but in actuality, it was invented by bartender Sam Ross in 2005 at Milk & Honey (now owner of Attaboy), a bar in New York City's Lower East Side.

YIELD: ONE SERVING

INGREDIENTS:

1.5 ounces Scotch (typically a blended Scotch, like Monkey Shoulder)

1 ounce lemon juice (freshly squeezed, if possible)

1 ounce honey-ginger syrup, or use equal parts (.5 ounce) ginger syrup and honey syrup (which is 1:1 honey and hot water)

INSTRUCTIONS:

Place all ingredients in a shaker with ice and shake.

Strain over fresh ice (if possible a large rock) in an old-fashioned glass.

Float (preferably spray) peated Scotch on top and serve.

Egg White Whiskey Sour

The recipe was featured in Jerry Thomas's Bartenders Guide (1862). *According to* The Alcohol Professor *magazine, Vice Admiral Edward Vernon of England invented the original sour recipe to help prevent his sailors getting scurvy.*

YIELD: ONE SERVING

INGREDIENTS:

1.5 ounces whiskey of choice

1 egg white

0.75 ounce lemon juice (freshly squeezed, if possible)

0.5 ounce simple syrup

INSTRUCTIONS:

Add all ingredients to a shaker and shake without ice first. Then add ice and shake.

Strain into a coupe glass and serve.

Split-Base Daiquiri

A daiquiri is a classic rum cocktail, invented in the late 19th century by an American mining engineer named Jennings Cox. Recently there have been many modern takes on it. This version splits equal parts rum and smoky whiskey.

YIELD: ONE SERVING

INGREDIENTS:

1 ounce overproof rum

1 ounce whiskey (preferably a smoky Scotch, like Kilchoman Machir Bay)

1 ounce lime juice (freshly squeezed, if possible)

0.75 ounce simple syrup

INSTRUCTIONS:

Place all ingredients into a shaker with ice.

Strain into a coupe glass and serve.

CLIMBING THE WALL

When nosing and tasting whiskey, it's not uncommon to experience the sensation of a heavy heat or burn when taking a sip, especially when it's your first sip of the day. Part of that is your palate acclimating to the alcohol, but for beginner drinkers, it may be attributable to not having experienced whiskey in the past. The key to getting past this burn is to slowly work your way up to drinking whiskey. Try it on the rocks, mix it with soda—whatever you have to do to be able to drink it at first—then slowly start working your way up to drinking it neat. Once you have climbed the "wall," or built up a tolerance to appreciate the taste of whiskey neat, then you can enjoy it in any other manner.

Tasting Whiskey

Now that you've professionally nosed a glass of whiskey and "climbed the wall," there are several different ways to really dig into tasting whiskey. My personal favorite approach is called the "Kentucky chew," which I learned from former West Coast American Whiskey Ambassador for the Jim Beam Distillery, Megan Brier (note that Brier learned it from 7th generation Beam family Master Distiller, Fred Noe).

The Kentucky chew takes a little getting used to but, in my opinion, is the best way to taste whiskey. First, nose the whiskey with your lips slightly parted and breathe in through your mouth. Then take a sip, but don't think about what you're tasting, just swallow it right away. Take the second sip after the burn from the first has passed, and this is where the magic begins. Take a nice-sized sip, not too big, and swish it all around your mouth. Get it everywhere, and I mean everywhere—under your tongue, in your gums, cheeks, teeth; everything should be coated in whiskey, because you want to "chew" on it.

Lastly, take one final sip. Hold it in your mouth for a second, then swallow. Smack your lips, then breathe out of your mouth. Do not breathe in, but rather breathe out. Doing it this way will allow a lot of the flavors of the whiskey to remain present.

You will likely taste lots of vanilla, caramel, oak, and toffee, which are common flavors in many whiskies. It depends, of course, on the type of grain. You can use the notes on flavors in each chapter to help you with your tasting. Once you have an understanding of the basic flavors to expect from each type of whiskey, you can then begin to look deeper for more notes and different subtleties of flavor. Remember, this process may seem strange at first, and whiskey may taste intense to beginners, so take your time to adjust to the flavors.

How to Read a Whiskey Label

The ability to read a whiskey label is a great skill to propel your understanding of what you're drinking. There is a lot of information on the label of a whiskey bottle. You expect to find obvious things like brand name, category, and proof, but the label also tells you what distillery it came from, if it's finished, what it's been finished in, its age, and sometimes even the mash bill. Let's break it all down.

Brand name: This will be the largest thing on the label. This isn't the distillery name, but the name of that particular whiskey brand. Some brands make several expressions using the same brand name. For instance, Garrison Brothers have four commercially available products and a few at the distillery only. George Dickel has BiB, bourbon with a few different age statements, and a rye.

Whiskey category: The category indicates what type of whiskey it is: bourbon, rye, single malt, single grain, Irish, etc. The category also tells you what country the whiskey is from. The label also includes the subcategory. For instance, for bourbon and rye, there are the subcategories straight and Bottled in Bond. For Scotch there is blended malt, blended grain, single malt, single grain, and blended. For Irish, there is pot still, single malt, single grain, and blended.

Finish: When a whiskey has been finished it will often say so on the label. For instance, let's say a straight bourbon whiskey's label states it is finished in Pedro Ximenez barrels. This tells us that the bourbon is a minimum of four years old and was then transferred into a barrel that formerly held Pedro Ximenez sherry. At this point, it is no longer legally bourbon, and the category becomes finished bourbon. It is a common practice in Scotch whisky to finish it in a second barrel, different from the one used for maturation. But with respect to Scotch, this does not change the legal classification.

Age: Distillers are not required to state the age of the whiskey anywhere on the bottle, but the whiskey must meet the aging requirements for the country of origin. For instance, in Scotland the requirement is three years. Bourbon has no minimum age, unless you are labeling it as a straight bourbon, in which case, it must be a minimum of two years old. However, if the bourbon is straight but does not list an age, it is required to be a minimum of four years old.

Some of the other items on the label may include alcohol by volume (abv) percentage, proof, volume, filtering, and tasting notes. Abv is the percentage of alcohol, which in whiskey is a minimum of 40 percent. Proof is double the abv. Volume tells you the amount. There are many different sizes, ranging from 50 ml to one liter (and occasionally 1.75 liters). Filtering designates whether the whiskey has been non-chill filtered or chill filtered. Chill filtration is when a distiller takes the whiskey down to an extremely low temperature (almost freezing) to solidify the lipids/fatty oils in the whiskey and filter them out. This will prevent the whiskey from getting cloudy under certain conditions or from the fats falling out of solution. Tasting notes are sometimes included on the back of the label.

The Key to Keeping Whiskey

Many of us have collections of whiskey at home, and often, we buy more than we drink. I know I'm guilty of having a collection of bottles that have remained unopened for years. Whiskey, unlike wine, does not continue maturing once you take it out of the barrel. As long as the bottle is sealed and unopened, however, it can last for several decades. It is likely with older bottles that the cork will begin to dry out, so if you do open the bottle years later, be careful. If you're looking to keep bottles of whiskey for years, keep them out of direct sunlight, ideally in a cool, dark place. If you want to avoid cork rot, you can rest the bottle on its side for a few days every so often, but for long-term storage make sure the bottle is straight up.

Once you have opened a bottle, the flavor will change over time. There isn't much you can do about it, aside from putting it in a smaller bottle each time. You can purchase a glass bottle with a swing top in many sizes so that you can reduce the size of the bottle as the volume of the whiskey decreases. The reason why you want the bottle to become smaller as the content decreases is that the more oxygen contact the whiskey has, the more the whiskey will change. Theoretically, you can keep a bottle of whiskey for years after it has been opened. Store it in a cool dark place and transfer it into smaller bottles as you drink so there will be less contact with oxygen.

CHAPTER 12

how to pair whiskey

One of the many ways to enjoy any spirit category is with a delicious meal, so in this chapter we will discuss some food pairing options for whiskey. I am not a culinary expert, so I collaborated with my friend, Chef Julian Maynes, who created fantastic dishes that we paired with selections from my personal whiskey collection and tasting library.

Scotch

The question here isn't what pairs well with Scotch, but rather what doesn't. Because of the vast differences in Scotch whisky producing regions, there is a dram for every meal. A nice smoky Scotch whisky, like a peated Islay, pairs really nicely with a piece of red meat like a steak.

Chef Maynes and I also discovered a great pairing in blackened chicken breast with bell peppers and a peated Highland Scotch whisky. While we found an Islay to be too aggressive in smoke for the blackened chicken, the balance of sweet and smoky in the Highland worked great. We also paired top sirloin and charred asparagus with a peated Scotch, this time from the Isle of Orkney, which played beautifully because of the heather and brine characteristics.

The best method to enjoy the pairings here is neat or in a cocktail that highlights the smoke, such as a Penicillin (page 111).

Irish Whiskey

The delicate balance of Irish whiskey works really well with dessert. The single malts have a nice roundness to them that pairs well with sweet and delicate flavors rather than big, bold, robust, savory ones.

Irish pot stills fare better with white meat such as chicken or pork.

Neat or on the rocks works best in this pairing. A cocktail would be too overpowering in this case.

Bourbon and Rye

Bourbon is such a vast category that theoretically it could pair with anything. Our recommendation is to play off the natural sweetness of the corn and go with something a little more flavorful like fish or barbecue.

A nice wheated bourbon, like Larceny, plays really nicely with pan-seared salmon. The sweetness from the salmon is mellowed by the wheat in the bourbon. Bourbon also works great as a glaze or as a part of a dipping sauce. At one bar where I worked, we used bourbon maple syrup, and I've even had bourbon in doughnut glaze (very addictive). Bourbon and vanilla ice cream are an excellent match.

Rye also pairs nicely with food that has pronounced flavors, like fish, and plays really well with vegetable dishes. What's more, the spice from the rye grain will really help cleanse the palate in between bites and prime it for the next course. We used a Sagamore Spirit cask-strength rye whiskey for this course and found that the higher abv added an extra spice and intensity that helped with intermediary palate cleansing.

For bourbon pairings, I would suggest a Gold Rush cocktail (which is similar to a Penicillin but without the smoke) or sipping it neat. For rye, neat really is the best way to go.

Canadian Whisky

As we discussed earlier, many of the products coming from Canada are rye-based spirits, which are often lighter and sweeter than American rye whiskies. Pairing Canadian whisky with a dessert such as vanilla ice cream or a tres leches cake works well.

For Canadian whiskies, I would suggest drinking them neat or with a couple drops of water, so as to release more of the flavor of the whisky. Alternatively, a cocktail like an Egg White Whiskey Sour (page 112) works nicely.

Japanese Whisky

Because a lot of Japanese whisky tends to be really soft and delicate while retaining a nice floral and fruity note, I recommend pairing it with sushi or sashimi, letting the soft notes of the whisky meld with the unadulterated flavors of fish. Alternatively, if you want to go on the opposite side of the spectrum, Japanese whisky also works well with a heartier dish like a burger.

For Japanese whisky, Chef Julian made salmon sashimi, brushed it with soy sauce, then lightly seared it. I paired it with Hibiki Harmony. The creaminess of the fish and saltiness from the soy sauce played well with the light notes of the whisky.

For this pairing I would suggest a highball style cocktail, with 1.5 ounces of whisky topped with club soda, over ice, in a tall glass. Neat works as well.

Tips for Hosting a Whiskey-Tasting Party

When it comes to figuring out what to pour for your guests at a whiskey-tasting party, there are two methods I recommend. The first method is that you decide what bottles to provide. I would suggest a minimum of three. They could come from your private whiskey collection, or you could go and purchase new bottles. Experiment. Mix up the categories. Just make sure you present the smokier/peatier options last so as not to corrupt the palate.

The second method is to do it potluck style. Give your guests a theme or general idea of what to bring and let them find something they think is going to be really interesting. This method is riskier, depending on how knowledgeable about whiskey your guests are. This could go really well, and they could bring really nice bottles, or they could opt to spend less and bring "rot gut" (bad or low quality alcohol).

Have guests take notes on the flavor and aromatics of the whiskey. Adding water is acceptable; just make sure to note that. At the end of the event, guests can vote on which bottle was their favorite and see how their palate progressed from the start of the tasting.

The food you choose to serve at your tasting party is a very important consideration. During the tasting itself, I would advise saltines only. They will help cleanse the palate and won't compromise flavors. Also, make sure to keep lots and lots of water on hand. If you use an external water filter, not one in your fridge, keep it filled at all times. Water bottles are also a great idea. After the tasting is complete, any food goes. In addition to food, cocktails are fun, but not a necessity. If you're going to go that route, do something easy like an Old Fashioned (page 110). You can either batch it ahead of time or make it fresh on the spot for your guests. If you're going to batch it in advance, just multiply the measurements by the number of people you expect, though it can't hurt to add a few more just in case.

Most important: When hosting a whiskey-tasting party, make sure your guests get home safely. Be conscientious about your friends drinking and driving home. Make sure they are okay to drive by ensuring that they're drinking water and eating. Have a spare bedroom available for anyone who really shouldn't be driving home (despite how much they insist). And remember, this is not you and your guests going out to the bar for a few rounds of drinks; this is a whiskey *tasting* and as such, the pours should be on the smaller side (I would recommend around ¼ to ½ ounce at most).

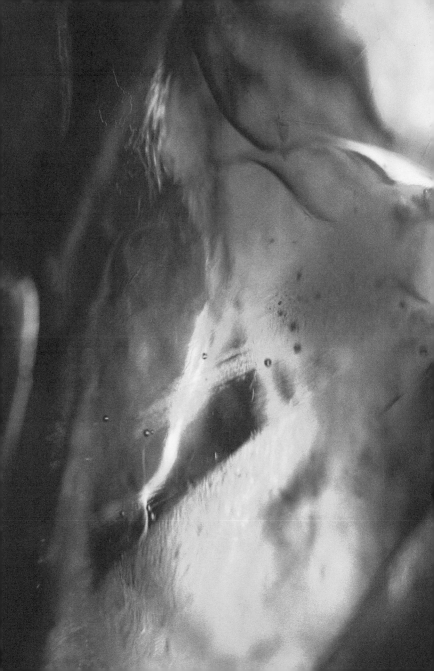

Sláinte!

AND WITH THAT, I've completed my ravings about whiskey. If you only take one thing away from this book, I really hope that it is the discovery of a new favorite. There are hundreds, if not thousands, of whiskey brands out there. If you think you don't like something, I suggest giving it one more try at a local bar. You never know what might be affecting your palate one day, causing you to dislike a whiskey you may otherwise fall in love with.

Often the really neat bottles go unnoticed because they're not from a "name brand." I encourage you to branch out and reach for something new. You never know when you might surprise yourself and find a new favorite. And when you do, please drop me a line with your latest discovery at sam@thewhiskeysomm.com.

To me, whiskey is about more than just what's in the glass. It's about community: the people who you share that whiskey with. It's about the people behind the bottle. If you join your local community of fellow whiskey enthusiasts to share bottles, swap tasting notes, and attend or host tasting events, your enjoyment will expand exponentially. One of my favorite things about whiskey is discussing it with the people who make it. It's always a great time when one gets the opportunity to talk to the distiller, the blender, or any of the people who work at the distillery. They are almost guaranteed to know the answers to your complex questions.

In my experience as a whiskey sommelier, training bartenders, creating menus, and interacting with distillers and ambassadors while hosting tastings both public and private, I have discovered that there are many fantastic paths to building a career in whiskey. I love what I do, and I wouldn't have it any other way. But the most important thing is that you enjoy whiskey how you want to enjoy it, be it as an occasional drinker, a passionate enthusiast, or a career-minded whiskey lover just starting out. And remember, the best whiskey is the kind of whiskey that you like to drink.

Sláinte,
Sam Green
Los Angeles, 11/16/19

Resources

THE FOLLOWING are some fantastic resources for learning about whiskey and the world of booze.

BOOKS:

Broom, Dave. *The Way of Whisky: A Journey Around Japanese Whisky.* London, UK: Mitchell Beazley, 2017.

Bryson, Lew. *Tasting Whiskey: An Insider's Guide to the Unique Pleasures of the World's Finest Spirits.* North Adams, MA: Storey Publishing, 2014.

MacLean, Charles. *Malt Whiskey: The Complete Guide.* London, UK: Mitchell Beazley, 2017.

Rogers, Adam. *Proof: The Science of Booze.* New York, NY: Houghton Mifflin Harcourt, 2014.

EDUCATIONAL COURSES:

The Whiskey Marketing School and Sommelier Program – WhiskyMarketing.org

Moonshine University Stave and Thief Bourbon Steward Program – StaveAndThief.com

The Edinburgh Whisky Academy – EdinburghWhiskyAcademy.com

WEBSITES:

The Spirits Business – TheSpiritsBusiness.com
Whisky Advocate – WhiskyAdvocate.com
The Whiskey Wash – TheWhiskeyWash.com

GLOSSARY

ABV: Alcohol by volume; the amount of alcohol to water in a spirit.

ANTI-SALOON LEAGUE: An organization that lobbied for Prohibition.

APPELLATION: Being of a place. Denomination of origin.

BLENDED MALT SCOTCH: Single malt from at least two distilleries in Scotland blended together.

BLENDED SCOTCH: Single malt and single grain from at least one distillery in Scotland blended together.

BOURBON: A whiskey distilled from a minimum of 51 percent corn. Can only be made in America.

BOTTLED IN BOND: A legally protected subcategory of American rye or bourbon whiskey. Bottled in Bond whiskey must be four years old at minimum and bottled at exactly 100 proof.

BRAND AMBASSADOR: The person who works for the company representing a whiskey.

BRANDY: A spirit distilled from grapes anywhere in the world. Cognac is an example of this.

COGNAC: A spirit distilled from grapes in the Cognac region of France.

CONDENSER: This is attached to the still, usually via the lyne arm, which helps cool the hot vapor back into a liquid.

CONTINUOUS STILL: Also called a column or Coffey still, invented by Aneas Coffey. This is used for continuous distillation.

CONTRACT DISTILLING: A variation of sourcing. This is when you partner with another distillery to create a new make for you to your specifications instead of just purchasing existing stock.

COOPER: A person who makes and/or repairs barrels.

COPPER POT STILL: A still designed for batch distillation. Its base is the shape of a pot.

DAVE PICKERELL: Former master distiller at Maker's Mark, founder of WhistlePig Whiskey. Affectionately called the fifth member of Metallica because of his work creating their whiskey label, Blackened.

DISTILLATION: The process of converting the distillers' beer/mash into a spirit.

DUNNAGE WAREHOUSE: An alternative style of whisky aging warehouse used in Scotland. Typically made of stone with bare earthen floors.

ENTRY PROOF: This is the proof (double abv) at which the spirit will enter the barrel.

FERMENTATION: The process of extracting the sugar from the malted grains through yeast and the creation of the distiller's beer.

FILL PROOF: This is the proof (minimum 80) at which the whiskey will be bottled.

FINISHING: The process of taking the already mature whiskey and placing it into another barrel to impart flavors from that second barrel; e.g. sherry casks, tequila casks, etc.

IRISH WHISKEY: Whiskey made in Ireland.

ISLAY: An island off the coast of mainland Scotland where most peated Scotch comes from.

KOJI: A type of mold that is often used to ferment soybeans. It is used in the fermentation of rice-based spirits, particularly in Japan.

LINCOLN COUNTY PROCESS: The process of charcoal filtering a new-make spirit. This is legally required for a whiskey to be labeled a Tennessee whiskey.

LYNE ARM: This is attached to the still and helps with reflux.

MALTING: The process of germinating the grains to allow the mashing process to extract sugar from inside.

MASHING: The process of cooking the malted grains.

(MASTER) DISTILLER: A person in charge of the distillation process.

NEUTRAL SPIRIT: Neutral alcohol, such as vodka, distilled to such a high proof that there is essentially no flavor left. Usually over 90 percent abv.

NON-DISTILLING PRODUCER (NDP): These are companies that don't distill their own spirit. They purchase and label it, often times to their own specifications. They do not have a distillery out of which to operate.

ORKNEY: An Island in the northern part of Scotland known for producing Highland Park single malt scotch whisky.

PEAT: A fuel source made of decayed/decaying vegetation, similar to coal; this generally gives whiskey its heavy smoke flavor.

POITÍN: Ireland's original, unaged spirit made from anything that could be distilled.

PROHIBITION: The prevention of the manufacture and sale of alcohol in the US between 1920 and 1933; made law by the 18th Amendment; implemented by the Volstead Act.

QUERCUS: This is the Latin word for oak. There are many different sub-species of quercus such as alba, robur, or mongolica.

REPEAL DAY: December 5, 1933; the day that the US government ratified the 21st Amendment, which repealed Prohibition.

RICKHOUSE: A whiskey-aging warehouse, typical in bourbon and rye production, where barrels are stored.

RUM-RUNNING: Also called bootlegging. The business of transporting, manufacturing, and selling illegal alcohol.

RYE: A whiskey distilled from a minimum of 51 percent rye grain.

SCOTCH: Whisky made in Scotland and aged for a minimum of three years.

SHOCHU: A rice-based liquor popular in Japan. This is usually distilled from sake.

SINGLE GRAIN SCOTCH: A whisky distilled from 100 percent malted cereal grains in Scotland. These can include barley, rye, wheat, and corn.

SINGLE MALT: A whiskey distilled from 100 percent malted barley.

SINGLE MALT SCOTCH: A whisky distilled from 100 percent malted barley in Scotland.

SINGLE POT STILL WHISKEY: A whiskey style unique to Ireland. Made of a minimum 30 percent malted and minimum of 30 percent unmalted barley.

SPEAKEASY: Originally a secret bar that popped up during Prohibition. One had to "speak easy" so as not to alert the authorities of the illicit activity taking place inside.

SPIRIT SAFE: An enclosed device used in the distillation of whiskey. Often, distillers will make their cuts here, directing heads or tails into a different receiver.

SOURCING: Purchasing spirit (either aged or new make) from another distillery, then bottling and labeling it as your own.

TENNESSEE WHISKEY: Whiskey distilled, aged, and bottled in the state of Tennessee. It must go through the Lincoln County Process to be called Tennessee whiskey.

TERROIR: The natural environment in which a whiskey is produced. This includes soil, climate, grain, etc.

UISGE BEATHA: From Scottish Gaelic; literally "water of life," this is the origin of the modern word "whiskey." Also "uisce beatha" in Irish Gaelic.

WASHBACK: An oak or stainless steel vessel in which distillers will ferment the mash.

WHISKEY/WHISKY: A distilled spirit from a fermented recipe of grains.

WHISKEY SOMMELIER: Similar to a wine sommelier (French for "steward" or "butler"). A person who was been trained in whiskey. Alternatively, someone who has gone through the whiskey marketing school program.

WOMEN'S CHRISTIAN TEMPERANCE UNION: An international organization of Christian women dedicated to social reform by means of advocating against tobacco, alcohol, and substance abuse; one of the organizations that helped to push Prohibition into law. The WCTU still exists, though they hold a fraction of the political influence they once did.

INDEX

Page locators in **bold**, indicate charts and illustrations

ᗩCKNOWLEDGMENTS

THE PHRASE "it takes a village" may be a cliché, but never have I felt it more than when I was writing this book. Everyone named here has been instrumental in my career, and their knowledge has filled any gaps in this book. Thank you!

To Dave Pickerell—While you may no longer be with us physically, you're still here in spirit. I miss you often, and the relationships I developed in part because of you are some amazing ones. I only wish I had taken the time to glean more knowledge from you before you passed.

To Raj Sabharwal—Thank you for taking the time to speak with me in regard to Indian whisky, and the drinking habits of the culture and country. It rounds out my knowledge to have insight into other cultures' drinking habits and products they produce.

To Rick Edwards—I really can't thank you enough for *all* the support and knowledge you've given me over the years. I do not call many people this, but you are a mentor to me. Even more importantly, your friendship means so much to me.

To Chris Uhde and Johnnie "The Scot" Mundell— Thank you both for lending me your time to go over

Japanese whisky and the aspects of Mizunara maturation about which I was unfamiliar.

To Jake, Allan, Bryan, Rachel and every other distiller or blender who has taken the time to talk to me about whiskey before and during the process of writing this book—thank you for your help, and for sharing your knowledge and passion for this liquid.

To everyone else who has supported me in my journey in the world of whiskey—thank you so much. It really means a lot to me. This book would really not be possible without all of you. There are too many to name, but please know I appreciate and respect you immensely.

ABOUT THE AUTHOR

SAM GREEN is a certified Bourbon Steward and a second-degree Whiskey Sommelier based in Los Angeles, California. His journey into the realm of whiskey and spirits started at the age of 22, and since then he has quickly taken his love of whiskey to new heights. His rapid ascent can be traced back to the same reason he entered the spirits industry in the first place: passion for and a bottomless curiosity about whiskey. He hosts private tastings all throughout the world and brings his boundless desire to learn and share whiskey with him wherever he goes.